MaryAnne O'D

March 20, 1996

# ECHO
## OF THE ELEPHANTS

# ECHO
# OF THE ELEPHANTS

*The Story of an Elephant Family*

Cynthia Moss

Photographs by Martyn Colbeck

William Morrow and Company, Inc.
New York

*For Marion*
*whose enthusiasm, talent*
*and friendship*
*touched so many of us*



Map on page 17 and diagram on page 32 by Eugene Fleury

First published in Great Britain in 1992 by BBC Books, a division of BBC Enterprises, Ltd.



Library of Congress Cataloging-in-Publication Data

Moss, Cynthia.
Echo of the elephants : the story of an elephant family / Cynthia Moss.
p. cm.
ISBN 0-688-12103-9
1. Echo (Elephant) 2. African elephant—Kenya—Amboseli National Park—Behavior. 3. African elephant—Kenya—Amboseli National Park—Biography. I. Title.
QL737.P98M667 1993
599.6′1′096762—dc20 92-33463
CIP

Printed in the United States of America

2 3 4 5 6 7 8 9 10

# CONTENTS

# ACKNOWLEDGEMENTS

Marion Zunz had a passion for life in its many forms. The natural world inspired and delighted her and no animal more so than the elephant. It was long her dream to make a behaviour film about African elephants based on the long-term research findings of the Amboseli Elephant Research Project. As only Marion could do, she persisted, gently but persuasively, for 10 years and finally her dream became a reality. In January 1990, with Marion as producer, we began a two-and-a-half-year project to make a film about the Amboseli elephants. Apart from two trips to Kenya, Marion encouraged us and followed our progress from the frustratingly distant BBC offices. Nevertheless, she got as involved with the EBs, 'our family', as we were. Marion did not live to see the final version of the film or book. She was killed in a skiing accident on 5 January 1992. It was Marion's energy, her intelligence, her unique off-beat view of things, her humour, and most of all her commitment that created the film and made this book possible. We have dedicated the book to Marion in appreciation for all that she did and was.

A film is always a team effort, and even a book, although apparently a more solitary undertaking, relies on the work of others. Many people and organisations helped us over the two and a half years of filming, post-production, writing and editing. First on the film production side we would like to thank the following for their invaluable contribution and support: David Attenborough, Martin Elsbury, Angela Groves, Christina Hamilton, David Heeley, John Heminway, Lesley Jones, Fred Kaufman, Ginny Lucas, Cathy McConnell, Linda Romano, Mike Rosenberg, Mike Salisbury, Marney Shears and John Sparks. The book benefited greatly from the efforts of the following: Sheila Ableman, Nicky Copeland, Harvey Ginsberg, Tim Higgins, Frank Phillips, Anthony Sheil

and Wendy Weil. We are also grateful to Jane Harvey and Chris Elworthy of Canon UK Ltd, Mecca Ibrahim of Fuji Professional and David Cottam of Fuji Film Processing for their generosity and skills, and to Wayne Esarove and Zenith Datasystems for their invaluable support.

Africa is not the easiest of continents to work on, but it has the friendliest and most helpful people. We could not have carried out our project without the aid of the authorities and our many friends and colleagues. We would first like to express our appreciation to the Ministry of Information and Broadcasting of the Government of Kenya for allowing us to film in the country, and to Richard Leakey and Joseph Mburugu of Kenya Wildlife Service for permission to work in Amboseli National Park. In Amboseli itself we owe a debt of gratitude to Warden Naftali Kio and Assistant Warden Michael Kipkeu for their hospitality and support.

In Nairobi we greatly appreciated the backing of a number of people: Billy Dhillon of Movietone Productions, Alison and Peter Cadot and the African Wildlife Foundation office, particularly Mark Stanley Price and Deborah Snelson. In addition, we also appreciated the enthusiasm and encouragement of Elizabeth McCorkle and Diana McMeekin of the AWF, Washington.

Our colleagues on the Amboseli Research Project and our companions in the camp were a source of encouragement and kindness and we would like to thank: Kadzo Kangwana, Wambua Kativa, Phyllis Lee, Keith Lindsay, Hamisi Mutinda, Peter Ngandi, Norah Wamaitha Njiraini, Joyce Poole, Deborah Ross, Soila Sayialel and Catherine Sayialel.

Finally, we would like to thank Conrad Hirsh and Heather, Josephine and Emily Colbeck: Conrad for providing an abundance of moral and material support in the form of supplies, communications, companionship, and, perhaps most important, his rescuing of us during the all too frequent vehicle breakdowns and disasters; and Heather and the girls for keeping the home fires burning and for their remarkable tolerance and patience during Martyn's long absences.

*Cynthia Moss*  *Martyn Colbeck*

# FOREWORD

## by Sir David Attenborough

I wonder if anyone has ever known a wild, free-roaming elephant as well as Cynthia Moss knows Echo. The two have been in one another's company for over 20 years now, sometimes for days and weeks on end. As Cynthia has watched, Echo has guided her family through good times and bad, finding food for them during famines, leading them on migration along traditional pathways, giving birth to her own calves and helping her sisters and daughters with the birth of theirs.

There was a time, not so long ago, when such a relationship between an animal and a zoologist would have been regarded with deep suspicion by orthodox science. For one thing, it might lead to an emotional attachment that could endanger scientific objectivity. Worse, it could result in that ultimate sin of the behavioural scientist, the unwarranted attribution to an animal of human motives and emotions. In any case, such arguments used to run, science should generalise not particularise.

Then things began to change. Watching animals in cages running round mazes and solving problems devised for them by experimenters became less fashionable. Zoologists abandoned their laboratories and moved out into the field to discover how animals

---

Overleaf: *A mother, her calf, and a younger female helper (all members of a larger family) head towards their night feeding and resting area as the sun sets. The matriarchal family unit is the basis of elephant society.*

behaved in their natural environments. There they realised that many questions could not be answered unless animals could be recognised as individuals. To do that, they used labels of some kind – collars around the neck, rings on the legs, even numbers tattooed or burnt on an animal's flank. This took time, was very laborious and might even endanger an animal's well-being, so it was difficult to do on a large scale. But a new generation of field-workers, with the keen observational powers of gifted naturalists, detected that individuals of many species varied enough in tiny physical details for them all to be recognised without having to interfere with them in any way.

That advance transformed the science of animal behaviour. As soon as observers began to follow particular animals over any length of time, they discovered that many of the generalisations made so confidently before were simply not true. All individuals of a species do not necessarily behave in the same way. Attributing particular characters to different animals is not always unjustified anthropomorphism. It may be an accurate assessment of the reality and bring a new understanding of the lives of many species.

No one animal could exemplify this more clearly than Echo. Her character emerges as vividly from these pages as might that of a human subject from a perceptive biography. And no longer is it a scientific slur to say such a thing. On the contrary, it is a tribute to Cynthia Moss's patience and insight as an observer. She has demonstrated that a scientist can be both objective and – using the word in its most literal sense – compassionate.

Today, elephants are in great peril. They are the biggest of all living land animals and as such they need great areas in which to roam and much vegetation on which to feed. In the increasingly crowded continent of Africa, there are more and more competitors for such things. To make matters worse, elephants carry in their jaws a treasure so valuable that there is a great deal of money to be made by killing them. If elephants are to survive, human beings will have to be convinced that these magnificent, intelligent creatures are entitled to retain some share of the living space left on earth. There could be no more persuasive argument for them than that provided by Cynthia Moss – and Echo – in this brilliant, perceptive and enchanting book.

# INTRODUCTION

Echo is not a particularly tall elephant nor is she perfectly proportioned, but nonetheless she is very beautiful. Her long, graceful tusks curve together and cross at the tips, and when she walks, she swings her head and tusks from side to side in a pleasing rhythm with her footsteps. Echo is the serene and gentle matriarch of a family of elephants that lives in Amboseli National Park in southern Kenya.

This book is Echo's story: it is an attempt to open a window into the life of one elephant family over a period of 18 months from January 1990 to June 1991. During many of those months, Martyn Colbeck and I followed, observed, photographed and filmed Echo and her relatives for a BBC documentary film on elephant behaviour.

## *Amboseli*

Echo's family, known by the codename 'EB', is one of 50 elephant families that live in and around Amboseli National Park. It is a small park by African standards, only 390 square

Overleaf: *Kilimanjaro dominates the landscape and ecology of Amboseli: rain falling on the mountain filters down into underground aquifers and surfaces in the Park in the form of springs, streams, swamps and pools, providing both food and water for an abundance of wildlife.*

kilometres (150 square miles), and much of it is the seasonally flooded bed of Lake Amboseli, which dried up 10 000 years ago. Receiving only about 300 millimetres (12 inches) of rain a year, the park should be a desert and the old lake bed does look as dead and dry as the Sahara for most of the year. Yet Amboseli is one of the richest wildlife areas in Kenya for the snows of Kilimanjaro glisten less than 40 kilometres (25 miles) away. Towering over the surrounding landscape at 5895 metres (19 340 feet), Kilimanjaro provides the lifeblood of Amboseli, continuously feeding the swamps and springs in the park with thousands of litres per minute of fresh, clear water carried in underground aquifers. The combination of low rainfall and underground streams makes the landscape of Amboseli a study of contrasts, with bare, dusty plains suddenly giving way to trees, papyrus and lush green swampland.

Amboseli's swamps and springs have been used by wildlife and humans and their domestic animals for hundreds of years. For the last 400–500 years, the area has been held by the Maasai tribe, fierce warriors and pastoralists who do not hunt wild animals for meat or trophies. The Maasai have lived in remarkable harmony with wildlife and, as a result, the best places to see wild animals in East Africa are those held by the Maasai. The oral history of the Maasai indicates that they have been sharing the Amboseli swamps with wildlife since they first arrived. Traditionally the Maasai and the migratory herbivores – elephants, buffaloes, wildebeests, zebras and gazelles – concentrate around the swamps in the dry season and disperse to outlying areas in the wet season. The dispersal area is almost 10 times as large as the park itself, up to 3000 square kilometres (1200 square miles), and without it the animals could not exist in the numbers that they do.

The Amboseli area has been visited by tourists since the 1930s and by hunters even before that. The wildlife was known to be easy to photograph and to shoot. In 1974, much of the central area around the swamps was declared a national park and the Maasai were asked to leave. In return they were given compensation in the form of a water pipeline and direct revenue. It has not been a completely successful arrangement, and periodically the Maasai spear elephants, rhinos and other large species, which is a traditional means

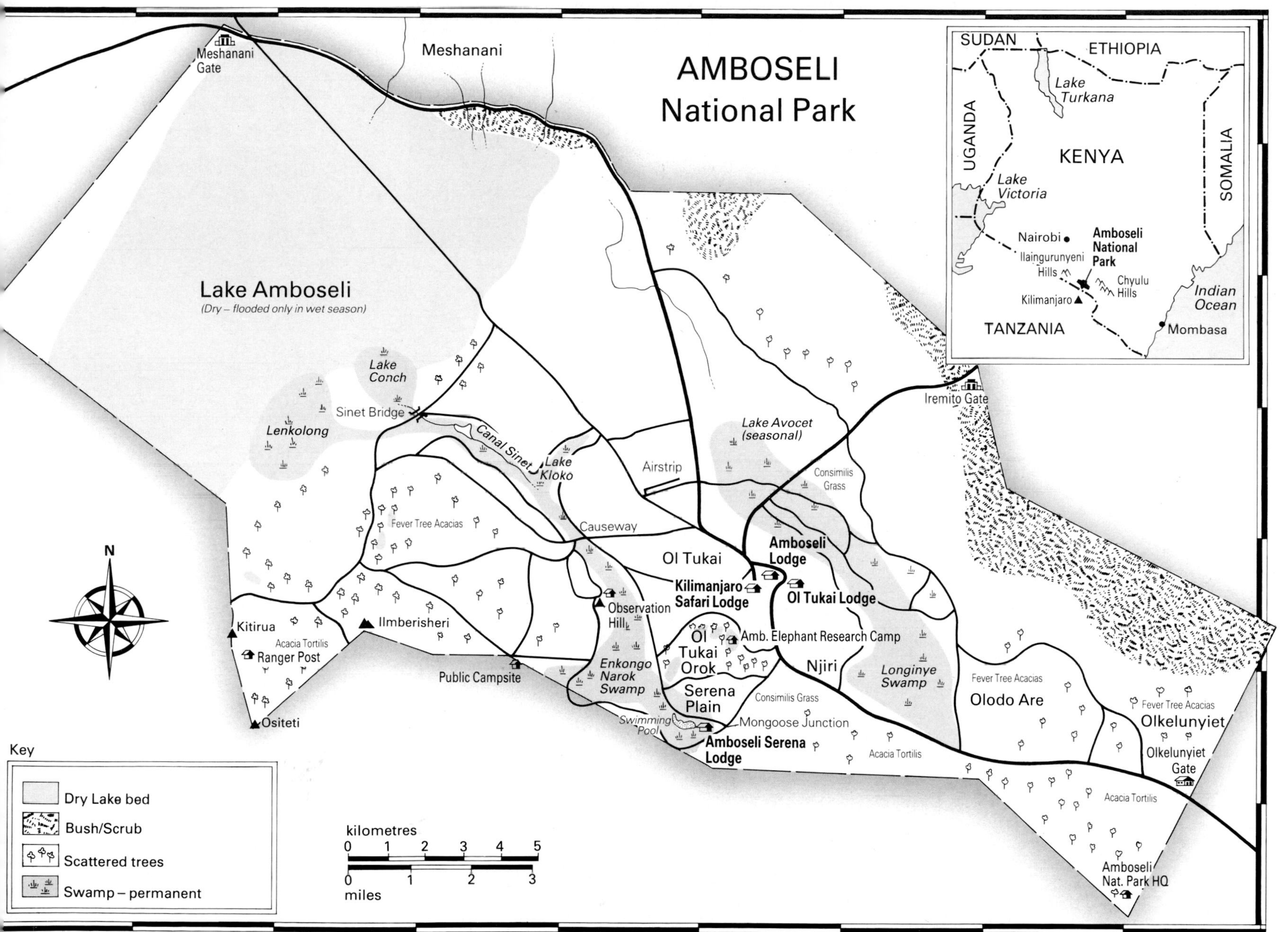

AMBOSELI National Park
Meshanani Gate
Meshanani
Lake Amboseli
(Dry – flooded only in wet season)
Lake Conch
Lenkolong
Sinet Bridge
Canal Sinet
Lake Kloko
Airstrip
Lake Avocet (seasonal)
Consimilis Grass
Iremito Gate
Fever Tree Acacias
Causeway
Ol Tukai
Amboseli Lodge
Kilimanjaro Safari Lodge
Ol Tukai Lodge
Observation Hill
Kitirua
Ilmberisheri
Acacia Tortilis
Ranger Post
Public Campsite
Ol Tukai Orok
Amb. Elephant Research Camp
Njiri
Longinye Swamp
Enkongo Narok Swamp
Serena Plain
Consimilis Grass
Fever Tree Acacias
Olodo Are
Fever Tree Acacias
Olkelunyiet
Ositeti
Swimming Pool
Mongoose Junction
Amboseli Serena Lodge
Acacia Tortilis
Olkelunyiet Gate
Acacia Tortilis
Amboseli Nat. Park HQ
N
Key
Dry Lake bed
Bush/Scrub
Scattered trees
Swamp – permanent
kilometres
0 1 2 3 4 5
0 1 2 3
miles
SUDAN
ETHIOPIA
Lake Turkana
UGANDA
KENYA
SOMALIA
Lake Victoria
Nairobi
Amboseli National Park
Ilaingurunyeni Hills
Chyulu Hills
Kilimanjaro
Indian Ocean
TANZANIA
Mombasa

Above and below:
*Elephants generally drink once a day, although in some seasons and in some habitats they can adapt to drinking every other day or even every third day. In Amboseli there is always enough water and, therefore, drinking sessions are relaxed and companionable occasions.*

*Mr Nick, an adult male in his mid-30s, moves across one of the large open pans in Amboseli. Males leave their families at around 14 years old to lead independent lives spending much of their time on their own or in the company of a few other males.*

of proving their bravery and, more recently, a form of political protest. Fortunately the incidents are relatively rare, and Amboseli continues to have an abundance of approachable and relaxed animals. It is also one of the few areas in all of Africa where elephants have not been under heavy pressure from poachers, mainly because the Maasai will not tolerate outsiders coming in to kill their wildlife.

## *The Amboseli Elephant Research Project*

The elephants of Amboseli are now the best known in Africa, having been the subjects of a detailed, long-term study which I initiated in September 1972 and have been directing ever since. I chose the Amboseli elephants for study because they were one of the last relatively undisturbed populations in Africa. My goal from the beginning was to collect basic information on elephants that were neither compressed into a small protected area nor heavily poached as most populations across the continent were. I hoped that data on elephants functioning in a fairly natural ecosystem, responding primarily to environmental rather than human-made pressures, would aid assessments of the status of less fortunate populations elsewhere. Sadly, the intensive poaching of the 1980s has made this role of the Amboseli project invaluable.

The Amboseli project is now in its twentieth year. With the help of colleagues, students and research assistants, I have been able to keep the study going continuously. Over 1200 elephants have been identified individually and each has been assigned a name, number or code. There are currently 755 living members, and well over half of these are known-aged – that is, their birth dates have been recorded to within one month. Their mothers and maternal sisters, brothers, aunts, uncles, nieces, nephews, and cousins are also known. Fathers and paternal relatives are more difficult to determine. Nevertheless, this fund of information on the histories and relatedness of the Amboseli elephants forms a unique body of knowledge for a wildlife population. It also makes watching them as fascinating as following a soap opera or reading an intricate family saga.

Elephant cows and their calves live in family units, which in Amboseli average about 11 members. A family consists of related adult females and their offspring, ranging from newborn calves to adolescent males and females up to about 10 or 11 years old. Families are tight-knit with strong bonds between the adult females. Each family is led by the oldest female – the matriarch. Female calves grow up and stay with the family, and may start producing their own calves at 12 or 13 years of age. Males leave the family soon after reaching sexual maturity at about 14 years old. They are then referred to as 'independent bulls'. Unlike the females, the bulls form only loose and temporary associations with each other. Usually it is the bulls over 30 years old who mate with the cows and father the calves.

In the Amboseli study, I catalogued males and females in different ways because of their different social lives. Since bulls do not form permanent groupings, each male has to be filed as an individual. Males have been assigned a number starting with the first bull that was photographed, M1. The numbers currently go up to M454 and are recorded on computer data sheets. There are presently 177 adult bulls, most of which have been given names as well. Females are filed according to family, and each family has an alphabetical letter code. At the beginning of the study, I assigned single letters to families but when I got to 27 I had to switch to a two-letter code, such as AA, AB, BA and BB. Each female is given a name starting with her family letter. Thus the AA family includes females named Amy, Abigail, Amelia and so on. For the data records, their names are shortened to a three-letter code, AMY, ABI, AME, etc. In Amboseli, the 50 family units are made up of 578 cows and calves.

Overleaf: *The EB family at rest with nine of the members visible (from left to right) Echo, Ella, Eric, Ewan, Edgar, Enid, Eliot, Eudora and Erin. At the beginning of 1990, the family numbered 14, which is just above average size for the 50 family units in Amboseli.*

Above and right:
*Echo, with her long, curved tusks, is very distinctive and very beautiful. She is also exceptionally gentle and non-aggressive, but at the same time a wise and experienced leader who has skilfully guided her family for at least 19 years.*

## *Family history: 1989*

Ninety eighty-nine started out well, with Emily giving birth to a male calf, Edo, in March. Then six months later an event occurred that would have profound repercussions in the family. On 8 September, Emily was reported missing yet Edo and his older brother, Emo, were still with the family. This situation almost certainly meant that Emily was injured or dead. My colleague, Joyce Poole, searched for Emily by car and by 'plane, and eventually found her carcass cloaked by a mass of vultures.

An examination showed that Emily had died not from a bullet or a spear but through human carelessness. There are lodges in Amboseli, and the people who run them do not always dispose of their refuse properly. Both elephants and monkeys are sometimes lured into the unfenced rubbish pits by food left lying around. One of the pits is near the EBs' main route to and from Longinye swamp. Emily's carcass was found less than 100 metres (330 feet) away from this pit. Her stomach contained bottle tops, glass, plastic, used batteries, and many other dangerous items, any one of which could have perforated her intestines. It was a terrible way to die.

Emily's death was the greatest trauma in this family's life since I had met them in 1973. The deaths of calves are no doubt distressing for their mothers, but the death of an adult female disrupts the whole family. As the second oldest female in the family, Emily was Echo's closest ally. She was also mother to Eudora, Emo and Edo, grandmother to Elspeth and a valuable 'teacher' for all the younger members of the family.

The most acutely affected member was, of course, Edo. The youngest orphan to have survived in Amboseli was 26 months old. At only six months old, Edo was eating some vegetation but he was still dependent on milk. He tried to suckle from his sister, Eudora, but she rejected him with persistence and force. Over the next two weeks he got thinner and thinner until all his bones stuck out and he became weak and lethargic. At this point, Joyce contacted Kenya's Wildlife Conservation and Management Department, which sent a team to capture Edo and take him to an elephant orphanage in Nairobi. After several

*Sitting in my blue Land Rover, I am accepted by the elephants in Amboseli as part of their environment. Since 1972 my colleagues and I have followed the histories of the individual elephants, recording the major events in their lives.*

weeks Edo recovered, physically at least. As I write this, he is in Tsavo National Park with other calves, most of which were orphaned by poachers. Eventually, they will be released into the wild.

In September 1989 when Edo was orphaned, I was in Nairobi where I was spending more and more time trying to draw the world's attention to the plight of the elephant. Poaching for ivory was putting the survival of all Africa's elephants in jeopardy. In October, I went to Switzerland to attend the Convention on International Trade in Endangered Species (CITES) conference at which, after a bitter battle, all international trade in ivory was banned. However, I knew the ban was not enough, that the only way to stop poaching was to reduce the demand for ivory, which meant increasing the public's knowledge of and concern for elephants. With this public awareness in mind, I travelled on to Britain

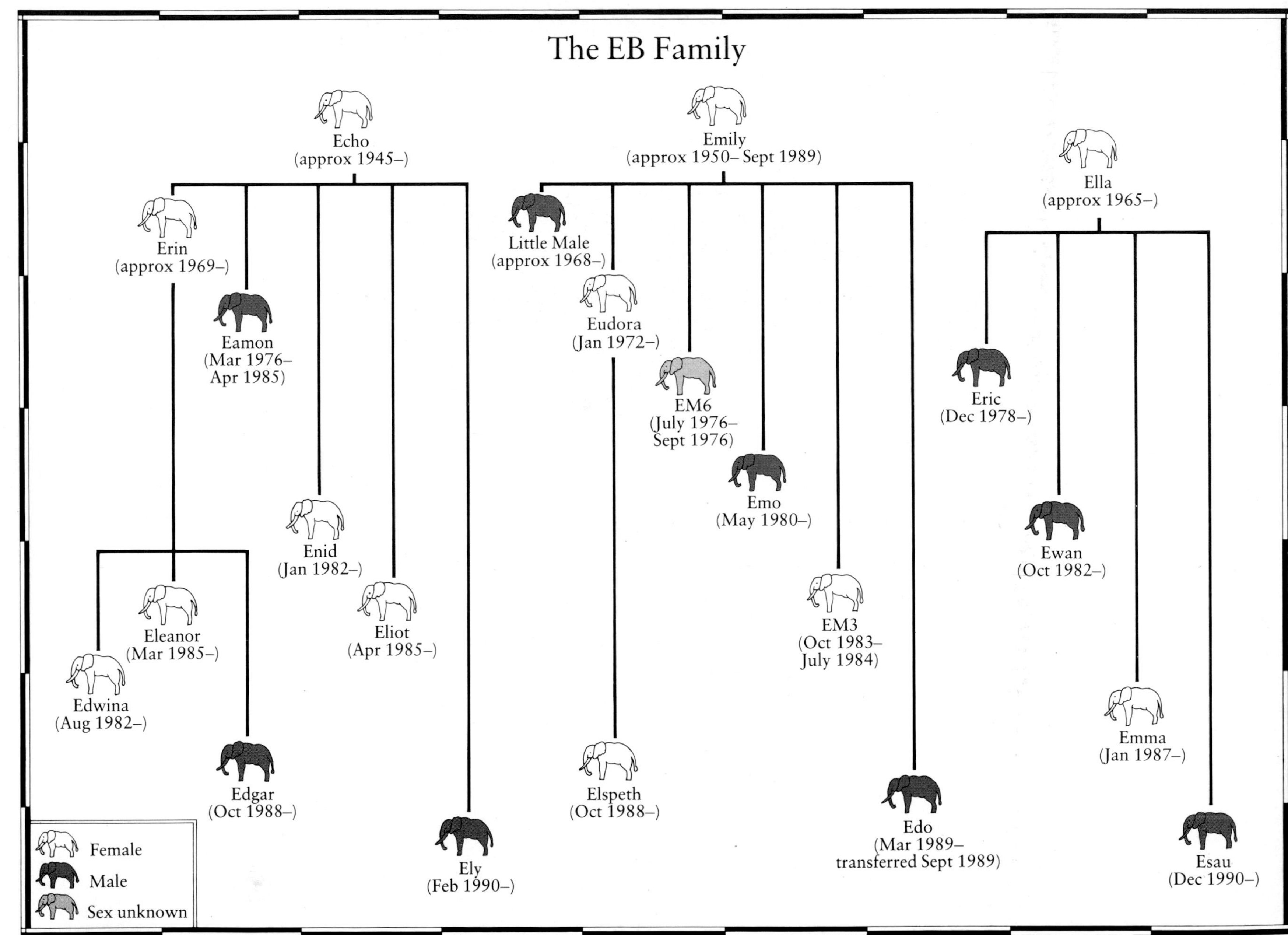
The EB Family
Echo
(approx 1945–)
Emily
(approx 1950– Sept 1989)
Ella
(approx 1965–)
Erin
(approx 1969–)
Eamon
(Mar 1976–
Apr 1985)
Enid
(Jan 1982–)
Eliot
(Apr 1985–)
Eleanor
(Mar 1985–)
Edwina
(Aug 1982–)
Edgar
(Oct 1988–)
Ely
(Feb 1990–)
Little Male
(approx 1968–)
Eudora
(Jan 1972–)
EM6
(July 1976–
Sept 1976)
Emo
(May 1980–)
EM3
(Oct 1983–
July 1984)
Elspeth
(Oct 1988–)
Edo
(Mar 1989–
transferred Sept 1989)
Eric
(Dec 1978–)
Ewan
(Oct 1982–)
Emma
(Jan 1987–)
Esau
(Dec 1990–)
Female
Male
Sex unknown

to discuss with the BBC plans for making a film about the daily life of a family of elephants in Amboseli.

At the BBC I met with producer Marion Zunz and cameraman Martyn Colbeck. I had known Marion for eight years and had great respect for her work. She had always been keen to do an elephant behaviour film with me and we had talked about it over the years. Then Marion and Martyn came to Amboseli in February 1989 to film the elephant sequences for David Attenborough's *The Trials of Life.* We worked well together as a team, and I felt that finally it was the right time and the right combination of people to do a full-length documentary on the elephants. We agreed to begin in January 1990.

On my return to Amboseli in late November, I quickly went in search of the film's prospective 'stars'. I located the EBs as they were crossing an open pan with Echo in the lead followed by her daughters, granddaughters, grandsons, nieces and nephews. It was sad not to see the 'head-low' Emily among them and I wondered how they would fare without her, particularly her daughter, son and granddaughter, Eudora, Emo and Elspeth. On this occasion, Eudora was in the main part of the group with one-year-old Elspeth, but Emo was trailing behind. Even when the family halted, he stayed 15 metres (50 feet) away, seeming hesitant to join them.

Sometimes when the mother of a young adult female dies that female and her calves become less integrated in the family and spend more and more time away from it. When the crunch comes, such as a drought, these are the members who lose out in the competition for the sparse resources. A female as young as Eudora would probably not do well on her own and the chances of Elspeth making it to adulthood would be greatly reduced. I would be watching to see what would happen to them over the next months. In the meantime, though, the EBs still appeared to be a tightly bonded family. Echo was a wise, old matriarch and I thought she would hold them together. As always I felt caught up in their lives and was greatly looking forward to spending the next 18 months with them.

# BETWEEN THE RAINS

## *January to early March 1990*

### *January*

Over much of Africa, it tends to rain during certain months, known as wet seasons, and for the rest of the year little or no rain falls. In Amboseli, there are two wet seasons and two dry seasons each year. A long wet season, the 'long rains', extends from mid-March to early June. From mid-June through to mid-October is the long dry season. Late October to early December is the short wet season or 'short rains'. Between these and the long rains is a short dry season, although scattered rain does sometimes fall from December to March.

The beginning of this short dry season was also the start of a new decade. I felt more optimistic than I did at the beginning of 1989 when African elephants were being poached at a terrible rate. Now there was an ivory ban, and I could relax my campaigning work and spend more time in Amboseli. I was particularly looking forward to observing a single family for long periods of time. I had, of course, spent thousands of hours watching elephants, but in a scientific study one must gather data on many elephants before drawing

*In typical EB-fashion, Eliot gazes calmly at the observer while Emma and Eudora stand unconcerned less than two metres from the vehicle. Their trust was the key to being able to enter and follow the lives of this family.*

Above: *The Research Project is based in a tented camp in a part of Amboseli called Ol Tukai Orok, a Maasai name meaning 'Place of the Dark Palms'.*
Below: *Elephants are individually identified by means of tears, holes, marks and vein patterns in their ears. Ella's right ear is easily recognisable.*

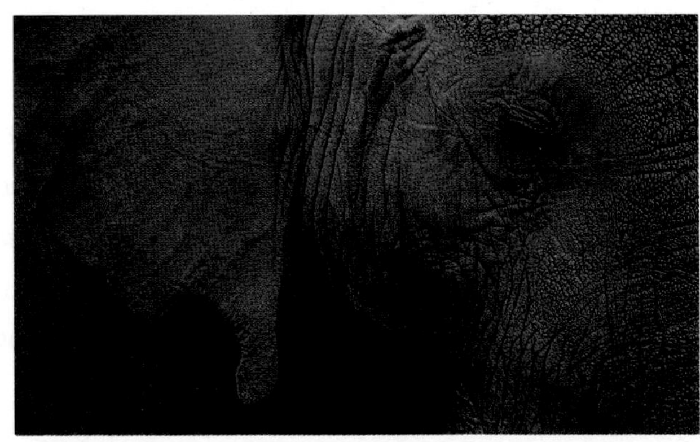

*When family members have been separated and meet again they invariably greet one another: Eudora (on the left) exhibits the typical greeting posture of head held high and ears spread as she backs in towards her family while vocalising, urinating and secreting from her temporal glands.*

Echo very rarely joined the big herds, preferring to lead her family along an independent path. At 45 years old, 20 years older than the next oldest female in her family, Echo was very much the matriarch. All the other members were aware of where she was and what she was doing. If they were resting and she woke up and moved off, they would move off. If there was a smell or sound of danger, they would look at her first and then act. If she called them with a low rumbling vocalisation they would come, and if she made the 'let's go' rumble they would follow. She was their core, their anchor, their leader.

Today they were feeding and moving, spread out in a loose but coordinated grouping. Each member was clearly visible, providing me with a good opportunity to start learning how to recognise them as individuals. I could already identify them when they were arranged before me like this. However, in order to tell the story of the EBs over the next year or so, I would have to become so familiar with each individual, including all the calves, that I could name them at a moment's notice under any circumstances.

An elephant's ears are its most reliable features for recognition purposes. By the time they are in their teens and twenties, many elephants have outstanding tears and holes in their ears. I am not sure how they acquire the injuries, but it is probably through catching their ears on thorns. Some elephants have much more ragged ears than others, presumably because they have thinner skin that tears more easily. Elephants with very smooth ears can be identified using photographs of the unique vein patterns on their ears. However, the veins are difficult to memorise and, anyway, might not always be visible. In these cases, additional distinguishing features and each animal's overall shape, posture, head carriage and gestures can be used.

I already knew the adult females well. Echo with her long curving tusks and U-nicks in her ears, and Ella with a big chunk out of the bottom of each ear were unmistakable. Erin and Eudora were less distinctive, but still readily identifiable. Echo's daughter, Erin, was remarkably similar to her mother in head and tusk shape, but had very smooth ears with no holes or nicks. Eudora had her mother Emily's narrow head and thin tusks, and she had a few small nicks in her left ear and a tiny hole in her right ear.

Of the three young males in the family, Eric, Ewan and Emo, Eric was the easiest to recognise. His ears were incredibly ragged, forming memorable patterns, and he had a short compact body. Ewan was no problem if seen head on or from his right side, because the top of his right ear folded forwards instead of backwards. When the EBs were all feeding up to their ears in the deep Amboseli swamps, it was often Ewan who gave them away with his folded ear showing just above the sedges. Emo was by far the most difficult of the larger animals to recognise away from the context of the family. Like his older brother Little Male, who had become independent several years before, Emo was the quintessential young male. He had very symmetrical tusks and hopelessly smooth ears, except for one tiny hole in the right ear, which could only be seen under the best of circumstances. But he did carry his head in a remarkably similar way to Emily and Eudora and, with practice, I thought I would soon be able to recognise him easily in any context.

Just as difficult as Emo were the five juvenile females. The youngest was Ella's three-year-old daughter, Emma. Then there were Echo's two daughters, seven-year-old Enid and four-year-old Eliot, and Erin's daughters Edwina and Eleanor who, confusingly, were also seven and four years old. Emma was the easiest because she was much smaller than the others with tusks about 7.5 centimetres (3 inches) long. I also noted that she had a small nick out of the top of her right ear. After her, the most distinctive juvenile was Enid who had splayed tusks which were longer than those of the other calves, and a small U-nick in the middle of her left ear. I recognised the other three calves by their foreheads, a feature I had never used before. Eliot was a veritable prunehead with many wrinkles, Eleanor had only two wrinkles across her head, and Edwina's forehead was perfectly smooth. Edwina also had a convenient bump behind her right shoulder.

The final two animals in the family were the babies, Elspeth and Edgar. They were just over a year old and looked exactly alike except that they were male and female. Fortunately calves of that age stick close to their mothers most of the time. It was only when they went off to play that they could be confused. Then I had to check on their sex, a method which got particularly tricky in tall grass.

As I was studying them, the family slowly wandered across the plain until they reached the edge of the Enkongo Narok swamp. In this area of the swamp there was a large pool of water covered in lily pads but free of thick reeds and papyrus. The elephants drank there and splashed themselves with mud. Afterwards, most of the family went on along the edge of the swamp but two of the young males could not resist the pool. Eric and Emo carefully lowered themselves down the bank and, like people painfully inching their way down a ladder into a swimming pool, they moved gingerly, one step at a time, into deeper water. When the water was halfway up their sides they started sparring and pushing

*Eric becomes a 'monster of the deep' as he plays in the elephants' swimming pool with his cousin Emo. Young males of Eric and Emo's ages (12 and 10) spend their spare time testing each other's strength and practising the skills they will need as adult bulls.*

each other. Eventually they fell or rolled over and submerged completely, coming up wearing ridiculous hats made up of the floating vegetation. Soon after, Edwina joined them and the three youngsters played for nearly an hour in the deep water. They pushed, shoved and climbed on one another, ran through the water smacking the surface with their trunks, stood in one spot kicking a front or hind leg violently backwards and forwards making huge splashes, and frequently sank completely with just the tips of their trunks showing above the water.

On the following day, 20 January, we had to spend a few hours tracking down the EBs. They are a relatively predictable group but the core area of their home range is still fairly large, at least 50 square kilometres (20 square miles). We finally found them at 10:15 in a big patch of elephant grass (*Sporobolus consimilis*) to the south of the Serena Road. They were with four other families, but soon Echo broke off from them and headed towards her favourite area, the Ol Tukai Orok woodlands. With the EBs went an adult male, 19-year-old Tolstoy, who had been born into the TD family and was now independent. I noted with interest that Tolstoy was bigger than the largest adult females. Males grow very fast during their teen years and continue growing throughout their lives. Females, on the other hand, grow more slowly in their teens and their growth nearly stops by the time they are 25. At that age, Tolstoy would be towering over the cows and in his 50s he might stand about 3.5 metres (11–12 feet) at the shoulder, while the biggest females would only reach 2.5 metres (8–9 feet).

As well as differing in size, adult males and females also live markedly different social lives. Females are rarely if ever alone, spending their whole lives surrounded by close relatives. The kin relationships among the females in a family are: mother and daughter, grandmother and granddaughter, sisters, aunt and niece, and cousins. They express their attachments by frequent touching of one another and by calling to one another with a wide range of vocalisations. There is a dominance hierarchy based on age, but more obvious is the cooperative behaviour such as mutual defence and the care of calves by members of the family other than their mothers, particularly adolescent females.

*When males leave their families they often join up with other bulls forming what could be considered as all-male clubs. These four males are all over 20 years old, but, with the exception of the bull on the left, they are not yet old enough to vie for the favours of females.*

Opposite: *Large adult bulls over 30 spend part of each year in 'retirement' and part in the pursuit of females. While in this retirement phase, a bull such as this one will feed and rest, building up his strength for the exhausting months of his active phase.*

*Eleanor was the first to come upon the bones of Emily, a family member who died in 1989. Elephants behave mysteriously around the carcass or skeleton of another elephant, often stroking and feeling parts of it, trying to bury it, or carrying off the bones.*

came into the Ol Tukai Orok swamps and woodlands in the daytime. However, this was proving to be an unusually wet 'short dry season'.

The extra rain was welcome both to the elephants and to Martyn and me. For the elephants it meant more food, for us it meant beautiful skies and no dust. All the elephants were fat and healthy, and had the energy and time to spend in social interactions. Almost every morning the calves had a long play session, sometimes chasing each other through the *consimilis* grass, other times ending up all in a heap on the ground in an attempt to climb on one another. A favourite game was chasing the hapless wildebeests that passed by. Two or three calves would go charging off, heads up, ears out, trumpeting shrilly, and the wildebeests would scatter in all directions.

The rains also meant that the elephants were more likely to wander out of their dry season home range. On 2 February we searched for the EBs throughout their normal haunts with no luck. Thinking that they had probably migrated again, we drove out west to the Ilmberisheri hills where we had found them before, and way beyond. Eventually, tired and discouraged, we gave up and returned to camp only to find them there, feeding peacefully in amongst the tents.

Our morning was not wasted, though, for we had come across Emo over to the west. He seemed to have taken a major step in the process of his independence, being over 20 kilometres (12 miles) away from his family. Emo stayed away for over a week, not returning to his family until 10 February. Probably because of my interest in Emo, I noticed several interactions between the adult females and the adolescent males in the EB family over the next few days. Little Ewan, who was only eight years old, got lunged at by Erin on one day and by Echo on the next. On the morning of the 13th, the EBs were resting out on the Serena plain, while Emo was standing alone under a tree 200 metres (650 feet) away. Later, he was moving with the family but keeping a discreet 30 metres (100 feet) away. A couple of hours after we had found them the next day, Emo arrived with a companion, Kyle of the KB family. Ella immediately turned on Kyle and chased him away. A few days later I saw Ella threaten Emo by folding her ears in a horizontal crease,

I was not surprised that Echo had abstained from frolicking in the water since, by my reckoning, she was over 21 months along in her pregnancy. Eudora's restraint had a less obvious reason, but accorded with her behaviour within the family since her mother Emily had died. I had been watching Eudora closely and found her strategy fascinating and not one I would have predicted. Instead of taking a subservient and peripheral position in the family, Eudora seemed to be trying to strengthen her bonds with Echo. In elephantine fashion, she was ingratiating herself. She stayed fairly close to Echo and every time Echo moved towards her, Eudora greeted her with a raising of her head and ears, and a deep, gurgling greeting rumble. On this one morning I saw her greet Echo more than a dozen times. The other two adult females, Erin and Ella, did not respond as conspicuously to Echo's approach unless they had been separated from her for a while. In turn, Eudora did not greet these two females in the same way, although her relations with them were amicable. A similar type of bonding probably goes on within families whenever an important adult member dies, but it was only through watching the EBs so intensively that I had gained this new insight into elephant behaviour.

I was now sure that Echo was pregnant and would soon give birth. Martyn and I had got so caught up in the anticipation that we were rather like doting grandparents, watching eagerly as Echo got fatter, her breasts fuller and she became slower and more lethargic.

I had concluded in my studies on oestrus and pregnancy that the average gestation period for elephants in Amboseli is 656. The 656th day from Echo's last recorded day of oestrus was 24 February. But, not surprisingly in such a long gestation, there is considerable variation and Echo could have her calf any time from mid-February to mid-March.

As 24 February approached it became more urgent that we find Echo as early as possible every morning. We had little hope of seeing the birth, because I estimate that 99 per cent of all births occur at night. The elephants are so relaxed around us that I think we would have seen dozens of births if they occurred in the daytime but in all the years of the study, my colleagues and I have only seen two births. Martyn and I wanted at least to see Echo's calf taking its first tottery steps and exploring its new world.

*Elspeth climbs onto Edwina, which is a favourite game of young calves. Older calves often invite these activities, but sometimes they are genuinely trying to sleep and find supporting 200 kilos of baby elephant a bit disturbing.*

---

We successfully located Echo every day until, on the morning of 24 February, we found ourselves in a dilemma. As we drove out of the camp, we came upon the EA family and saw that one of the females, Elvira, was in oestrus. Since we knew that, among the EBs, only Eudora might come into oestrus over the next year or so, we had decided to film an oestrous female in the same bond group if we were lucky enough to find one. There was Elvira being hotly pursued by bulls, while elsewhere, Echo's newborn calf might await us. So for the next three days we raced out at the crack of dawn, searched for the EB family to check on Echo, and then attempted to find the EAs and follow Elvira for the rest of the day. This was gruelling and not entirely successful, because we lost Elvira on one of the days, but we did manage to see her mating. Fortunately, by 27 February Elvira seemed to be out of oestrus and Echo had not yet given birth. That evening we observed her moving with the EBs along the edge of the palms, looking very tired and very large.

On 28 February we left the camp just as the sun was beginning to rise on a beautiful, clear morning, and headed down the bumpy, dusty road. At the Serena Road turnoff, a cheetah walked nonchalantly down the side of the road with 20-odd minibuses trailing it. We stopped briefly at what I call Mongoose Junction and watched a dwarf mongoose pop out of a hole in a termite mound, look around and then busily start grooming itself. From the junction we could see a group of elephants to the north across the open plain at the edge of Ol Tukai Orok, very close to where we had left the EBs the night before. We drove towards them and I could see that it was, indeed, 'our' family. Echo and her two daughters, Enid and Eliot, were standing to one side, and between Echo and Enid was a small object – the baby had come!

As we approached, the young male Tolstoy came over to Echo and leaned his tusks and trunk on her back, making a nuisance of himself. Echo still had blood on the insides of her hind legs and the birth fluids do sometimes appear to excite males. Echo moved around trying to avoid him, and the calf was hidden amidst all the legs and feet. When I glimpsed it again it was 'kneeling' on its front legs, with its backside facing the car, and I could see that it was a male. I thought the calf was probably two or three hours old, born in the last hours of the night.

We were so busy recording the scene that it was a few moments before I felt the first pangs of anxiety. I checked with Martyn and found that neither of us had seen the calf up on all four feet since we had arrived. Although he was shuffling round a bit, the calf was still 'kneeling' on his carpal joints (the first joints of the front legs, equivalent to our wrists). In the two births we had witnessed on the project, the calves were standing within

15 minutes of being born. I had observed many calves who were only a few hours old and all had been able to get up on to their feet. This calf's joints were covered in dirt and he had clearly been kneeling for some time.

Five minutes passed, during which Tolstoy wandered off and the calf continued on his knees. In turn, Echo and Enid wrapped a trunk around the baby and gently tried to lift him. He was an exceptionally large and robust calf, and very active. He reached up and tried to suckle from Echo or Enid, searching in the wrong areas – back legs, sides, front feet – as all newborn calves seem to do. After another 20 minutes, Eliot started to follow the rest of the family, which had disappeared through the palms heading north. Then she came back, obviously torn between staying with her mother and following the rest of the group. Five minutes later she went, rumbling, trumpeting and running at full speed to the north, leaving Echo, Enid and the baby behind.

The three of them were out on the open pan in the bright, morning sunlight. Scanning the clear views all around, I spotted the placenta glistening red on the ground about 30 metres (100 feet) away and realised that the calf had hardly moved at all. It was then, I think, we fully acknowledged that the calf had never been on his feet and that there was something seriously wrong with him. Soon two tawny eagles also spotted the placenta and dived down to feed. Dozens of vultures descended within minutes and the air was full of hissing and cackling sounds as they fought over the rich afterbirth.

I watched the calf carefully when he lay down on his side or on his brisket. His feet were bent back completely at the carpal joints which seemed fused in place with no flexibility whatsoever. With one exception, he was the biggest newborn I had ever seen, and I wondered if his large size had caused him to be cramped in the womb, forcing his feet to grow that way. I knew he could not survive for long with his legs bent. Even if he could shuffle along, his 'knees' would soon become raw and infected, and before that, he would die of hunger.

I was wrong about the hunger. At 9:00, through what looked like pure willpower, he found Echo's breast and managed to suckle. Newborn calves often have a difficult time

Below and opposite:
*Ely was born with the first joints of his front legs, the carpal joints, bent back and totally immobile. Echo and his older sister Enid tried to lift him to his feet and encourage him to walk, but he could only 'kneel' and move short distances by shuffling along.*

reaching their mother's nipple. They almost have to rear up on their hind legs, especially those calves that are small and have relatively large mothers. Echo's calf was both strong and tall, and by tilting back and stretching way up he could just reach. I was amazed by his success and also appalled. Convinced that he would die, I felt his ability to get nourishment would only prolong the agony for him and Echo.

For the next couple of hours, Echo kept trying all the things a mother elephant does to get a newborn calf up and on its feet. Every time he lay down, she would prod him with her foot and lift him with the aid of her trunk and foot. Sometimes he screamed the hoarse, deep cry of a distressed calf. When he got up in his kneeling position or tried to suckle, Echo would take a few steps away from him, encouraging him to move. He either stayed put or shuffled forward before collapsing again. Enid also tried to help him up and it was fascinating to watch Echo's behaviour towards her. At first she allowed Enid to prod the calf and try to lift him but later she began to push sideways with her tusks, gently moving Enid away from him. There was no aggression in the movement, which was always done carefully and slowly. While they stood over the baby, Enid frequently reached her trunk up to Echo's mouth, appearing to seek reassurance or information.

At 11:00 they were still out on the edge of the pan in the hot sun having moved only about 20 metres (65 feet) since we had arrived. Both Echo and Enid were flapping their ears at a high rate in an attempt to keep cool. They must have been very thirsty, particularly Echo after the efforts of giving birth. Occasionally, Echo would rumble a contact call and then hold still and listen. We could not hear any responses but she seemed to. Just after one of these calls, Enid rumbled and walked about 10 metres (33 feet) away from Echo and the calf, heading in the direction the family had taken. She stood rumbling with her back to Echo but with her head turned, watching her mother and brother. Then Echo once again tried to get the baby to his feet. He screamed, and Enid whirled and came back to him at a full run, and felt and stroked him with her trunk. She went off twice more, but each time came running back when the calf cried out. It was amazing how strong her instinct to care for her brother was.

Half an hour later, Enid walked over to a small waterhole and splashed mud over herself, and again ran back when she heard the calf. Just after noon, Echo got the calf up with some rough prodding and he crawled along behind her. During the next 20 minutes, they managed to move about 15 metres (50 feet) to a small swampy waterhole where both Echo and Enid splashed themselves with mud, getting the calf wet in the process. The calf lay down with his trunk half in the water, emitting a gurgling sound with every breath. Echo dug in the waterhole, waited for water to gather and drank three trunksful. Then she came out of the hole, and the calf got up and managed to suckle for the second time. It was obviously going to take a lot more than the hot sun and a little mudhole to finish off this strong, determined calf. I kept willing his feet to straighten, but they remained as rigidly bent as ever.

After their mudsplash and token drink, the three animals began to rest standing at the edge of the woodlands. Martyn and I left them at 13:30 and went back to the camp for lunch, but I could neither eat nor drink anything. Hours of watching the calf's gallant struggles and the distraught behaviour of his mother and sister had left me completely drained. I went over to see the park warden and reported that a malformed calf had been born. He listened to the facts and decided that no interference was called for.

In general, Kenya has a policy of non-intervention in its national parks. For example, starving lion cubs are not fed, and sick animals, unless they are a highly endangered species such as the black rhino, are not treated. I fully support this policy, believing that we should not meddle with natural populations and natural processes, but it doesn't make it any easier to sit and watch a crippled elephant calf trying to struggle to its feet or the distraught behaviour of its mother and older sister trying to help and encourage it. Taking everything into account, I still felt that I should confer with the Kenya Wildlife Service (KWS) authorities in Nairobi, particularly with a veterinarian. I had to see Richard Leakey, the Director, on another important matter, and I decided to travel to Nairobi the next day, while Martyn stayed in Amboseli to follow events.

At 15:00 Martyn went out with my assistant, Soila, and I joined them later. Echo,

Enid and the calf had moved about 30 metres (100 feet) and were standing near a larger waterhole where Echo had presumably been able to drink properly. The calf was lying down looking weak and exhausted, and we thought that, despite all his striving, he might die very soon. After watching them for a while, I reluctantly returned to the camp to pack. Martyn arrived back before dark, very depressed. He said the calf had slept for most of the afternoon, but had suckled again. Towards late afternoon rain, presaged by the particularly intense heat at midday, had begun to fall. I did not know whether the rain would help or hinder the calf.

The next day, 1 March, Martyn went out early with my other assistant, Norah, and returned just as I had finished packing up the vehicle and was about to leave for Nairobi. He had found the EBs, and the calf was still alive and shuffling along fairly well. Martyn also reported that one of the calf's feet seemed to have the tiniest bit of movement. Although he added that this was probably wishful thinking, the ray of hope stopped me forsaking my principles, and I did not call the KWS vet when I got to Nairobi.

Martyn kept a detailed diary while I was away, and the following are direct quotes or summaries of his notes, starting from the morning of 1 March:

We found Echo, Enid and the calf not far from where we left them last night. The calf was standing but still on his 'knees'. He looked stronger than he had at the end of the previous day. Perhaps he had benefited from the cool night. As we sat and watched in the dull, morning light the calf slowly followed Echo and Enid. He rarely lay down and continually tried to suckle. He seemed to be succeeding at times but it was an extreme effort. The only way he could reach the nipple was to sit down on his backside. In this way he could tilt at a sufficiently steep angle to reach the breast. We could tell when the calf was succeeding by the loud slurping sounds.

---

*On the second day, Ely had some flexibility in his carpal joints and was better able to reach Echo's breast and suckle, but he was still hopelessly crippled. Nevertheless, Echo and Enid watched over him and patiently geared their movements and pace to his.*

In the course of the morning other elephants came and went, and inspected Echo and the new calf. Later, the rest of the EB family arrived and performed a highly vocal and exuberant greeting ceremony. They raced over to Echo with their heads up and ears flapping, rumbling and trumpeting and then turning and backing towards her and the calf. Every elephant's temporal glands were streaming with excitement.

After coming back to camp in midmorning to see me off, Martyn and Norah spent the rest of the day with Echo, Enid and the calf. The family had wandered off again, and Echo moved a bit farther into the palms. At the end of the day Martyn wrote:

> One scene stays vividly in my mind. The threesome were heading towards us through the picturesque palms of Ol Tukai Orok. As the two older elephants walked, they continually turned to look back at the calf which was shuffling along behind. Every few feet they stopped and waited for him to catch up before moving on. Their progress was very slow, but they did not show any signs of impatience with the calf. It was a poignant sight and highlighted the incredible, caring nature of these animals.

On 3 March, Martyn went out with Norah at first light and after some searching they found Echo, Enid and the calf deep in the palms. They sat and waited until Echo emerged with the calf following on his knees. Martyn then went on to relate:

> Enid came last and when they got out into the open, they paused to feed. It was at this point that we first noticed something both unexpected and extraordinary. The calf was kneeling beside Echo when he suddenly started to try and lift himself up on to the soles of his front feet. I had to double check that what I thought I was seeing was actually happening, and sure enough it was. There *was* flexibility in the front joints; the calf *was* trying and partially succeeding in getting up on to his front feet! I was ecstatic, elated and suddenly full of optimism for the calf's survival and well being.
>
> We followed them out to a clearing where they rested for a while, at least Echo and Enid did. The calf proceeded to give us a display of sheer determination and guts. As Echo rested, the calf shuffled forwards towards the breast. He then leaned his body backwards until his two front legs were almost straight. Carefully and ever so slowly he transferred his weight back towards the front

*On the third day, in a tremendous feat of determination and persistence, Ely stood on all four feet for the first time. There were some falls and further struggles, but from that moment on he never looked back.*

end of his body and simultaneously straightened all four legs. He started to stand, but then oops, down he went on to his 'knees' again. The other elephants remained still as the calf repeated the whole slow and probably painful procedure. Each time he tried to stand his little legs would shake with the effort. We were willing him on as he tried again and again. Finally he straightened to his full height and stood wobbling precariously. He started to take a step forward to reach Echo's breast, but as soon as he lifted one foot, down he went. Undaunted, he stretched, stood and fell, over and over again. But what incredible progress since yesterday!

It rained hard in Amboseli on that afternoon and when Martyn and Norah went out the following morning it was wet everywhere and some portions of the roads were flooded. The rainy season had definitely arrived. Martyn recorded:

We found the whole EB family at the north end of Ol Tukai Orok. Of course, the first elephant that we looked for was the calf and sure enough he was there. We quickly realised that he was looking much stronger and incredibly he was *walking*! His legs were supporting his weight and, unlike yesterday, he was actually moving forward and staying on his feet. The carpal joints would threaten to buckle beneath him but he now had the strength to hold himself up and prevent himself crumpling into a kneeling position. As the others rested, the calf stumbled, limped around and suckled. We now wanted him to take in as much nourishment as he could, unlike when he was first born and, with sadness, we wanted him to fail. He even spent some time using his right front foot to play with a log. He appeared to be trying to stretch his foot by flexing it against the log.

Eventually the others started to move off and feed. The calf was better able to keep up with the rest of the family as they fed. It would not be long before the family would have to make no allowances for him. They did not move very far during the morning but, whenever they did, the calf was right there with them.

When Martyn rang me on 3 March, I knew just by the way he said hello that he was going to tell me something wonderful. His news exonerated any guilt I have ever felt for not interfering in a natural population of wild animals.

On 4 March, Martyn phoned again to tell me that the calf was walking well and showed little sign of the limping and stumbling of the day before. He suckled, walked, lay down and got up again like a typical few-days-old calf. Overjoyed, I decided to name the miracle baby. I wanted to call him Easter for his rebirth, but thought it might offend some people. In the end I settled on the first name that had come into my mind when we realised that Echo was going to have a calf: Ely. It was short and simple – and I had used up almost every other 'E' name in my five 'names for babies' books plus a dictionary of saints.

The next day, my meetings completed, I went to the African Wildlife Foundation (AWF) offices to try to find out more about Ely's condition. Gary Tabor, a vet who had recently joined AWF, had never come across the problem but searched his medical books for me. From my description, he decided that Ely had had 'flexure of the pasterns'. Although this condition was known in domestic livestock, including horses, it had never before been observed in an elephant. It is thought to occur when the dam is disproportionally smaller than the sire and the calf is relatively large. So my initial hypothesis was correct: because Ely was exceptionally large, his legs were scrunched up in the last stages of Echo's pregnancy and completely stiff by the time he was born. I also talked to the Director, Mark Stanley Price, who had seen the condition once in an oryx calf in Oman. Interestingly, he too had had to wrestle with his conscience over whether or not to interfere. He did not and that calf, a female, went on to be a very successful breeder in the herd.

Frustratingly, I had to wait until 7 March before I could get on a flight back to Amboseli. As we flew low to land, I could see a small group of elephants in northern Longinye with my Land Rover parked nearby. Norah and Soila, who were at the airstrip to meet me, reported that the EBs had moved over to Longinye the day before, which meant that Ely had walked a good 3 kilometres (nearly 2 miles) at least. Martyn soon joined us and we all went off to see the family. By the time we got there the EBs had gone into the swamp reeds but I could see little Ely ploughing through the mud and water with strength and energy. I felt like cheering for him.

# THE RAINY SEASON

## *March to May 1990*

### *March*

In most years the long rains did not get going until well into April, but by early March they had truly come. It was a welcome change. One only needs to live in the drier parts of Africa for a couple of years to become acutely aware of the importance of rain. Not only does it permeate the soils, it permeates the very spirit of the people and animals of Africa.

The rainy season washes everything clean and provides spectacular skies with something different going on in each quarter. From the flat, ancient lake basin of Amboseli there is a panoramic view of the sky. It is often possible to look west and see a brilliant blue sky, to look north and find huge cumulus clouds forming, to look east and watch a slate-grey storm approaching, pierced by the arc of a rainbow, and finally to see the tip of Kilimanjaro rising above whirling clouds to the south.

The rainy season is also a time of well-being because the rains bring up grasses, herbs and shrubs that supply an abundance of food for all the animals. In Amboseli, the coming

*Storm clouds build in a spectacular Amboseli sky: with only 300 mm falling in the Park each year, rain is precious and always welcome.*

of the rains heralds a dramatic change in the movement patterns of many of the herbivores. The elephants, buffaloes, zebras, wildebeests and Grant's and Thomson's gazelles are migratory species. In the dry season they concentrate around the Amboseli swamps for both water and food, but as soon as it rains most of these animals leave the basin and move out on to the surrounding higher ground, where the red soils produce more nutritious and palatable vegetation. In the case of the wildebeests and zebras, the departure is often very dramatic. One day the park might be so full of these grazers that it seems almost like a barnyard. The next day, after one night's rain, the park might have emptied with not a wildebeest or zebra in sight.

The elephants used to leave almost as rapidly as other migratory herbivores, but in more recent years they have tended to stay closer to the park. The change occurred in 1977 after the Maasai moved out of the park completely. The elephants rapidly learned where they would meet Maasai and where they would not, and a few spearing incidents each year keep them wary. The elephants still move in and out of the park but much of their feeding outside takes place at night when the Maasai and their cattle are in their *bomas* (thorn enclosures).

Nevertheless, there remain distinct seasonal differences in the daily routines and association patterns of the elephants. In the dry season there is little mingling of the families, each tending to move on its own within its clan range. A family will leave the basin at night, feed and sleep in the bushland to the south or east, and gradually come back to one of the swamps in the daytime. Families may feed near each other for a few hours in the daytime, but in the evening they usually separate again. The bulls, too, generally stay out in their bull areas and only rarely visit the families.

When the rains come, there is usually a lag of at least a week, while the vegetation responds to the rainfall, before the elephants abandon their dry season routines. But from the moment the rains start there is a restlessness among them, revealed by an increase in interactions and vocalisations. Soon families start coming together in larger groups of 40, 50 or 60 animals, including bulls who have joined the cows and calves. These groups might leave their dry season range and move to areas with the best vegetation. There they will probably meet other families from other clans and the other subpopulation. In years of high rainfall, aggregations of over 500 individuals might form.

It is at this season and in these large herds that elephants are at their most social. For the adults it is a time to re-establish bonds, meet old rivals, settle dominance ranks, and find suitable mates. For the youngsters it is an important time of learning through watching the adults, meeting age-mates and testing one another. Observing one of these big herds is rather like watching a continual party. In one section, two families could be performing an exuberant greeting ceremony and in another, calves might be playing in a great heap of wiggling trunks, feet, legs and ears. In the middle of the herd, three pairs of young males might be having vigorous sparring matches. On the edge, several bulls might be chasing a female in oestrus, while nearby, two bulls in musth could be starting a fight.

When I returned to Amboseli on 7 March to find Ely walking well and moving with his family, the elephants had already begun to exhibit their migratory urge. They were gathering and travelling outside their usual ranges, and we knew it would become increasingly difficult to keep track of the EBs and Ely.

The following day we went over to northern Longinye to the place we had seen the EBs the day before, but there were no elephants in sight. We drove across the plains and past a hyena den which, on inspection, showed signs of recent use. Then we went on into an area called Olodo Are (place of red water) by the Maasai, which is to the east of Longinye swamp and well out of the EBs' dry season home range. After a bit of searching we found them just at the edge of Olodo Are in one of my favourite parts of the park. This area consists of a long strip of *Acacia tortilis* woodlands, fronted by a sward of thick green grass interspersed with white-flowered shrubs. Rising behind the trees and forming an amazing backdrop are the dark greens, blues, purples and glittering white of Kilimanjaro.

On this morning, over 200 elephants were dotted about in a loose aggregation, some resting, some feeding, some already moving towards Longinye. Not surprisingly, the family the EBs were standing closest to was their fellow bond group member, the EAs.

*The coming of the rains and the ensuing growth of new vegetation mean that elephants have more time and energy for socialising and play.* Above: *Two young adults, a male and a female, gently trunk wrestle.* Right: *Three of the youngest EB calves start to climb on Edwina, who in this case lay down to initiate the play.*

Soon after we arrived they all began to move towards Longinye. The EBs and EAs started across the open pan with Echo striding out in the lead and Ely hurrying along beside her. He was doing very well, only a little unsteady on his feet. As they got close to the swamp, the ground dropped off and he stumbled on to his knees going down the slope, but he got up immediately and raced on. The elephants were moving fast at that point, possibly because they were thirsty and wanted to drink. The EBs had travelled a long way from northern Longinye the night before, a minimum of 7 kilometres (4.5 miles) and probably

*Rain also brings mud: Ely and Enid seem to be trying to get as dirty as possible, but their activity has a purpose; mudwallowing cools the elephant's body and coats it with a protective layer of natural suntan lotion.*

*Echo with her two youngest calves, Ely and Eliot. In a rare moment while her older sister is occupied elsewhere, Eliot is able to 'allomother' her younger brother. Juvenile females appear to be irresistibly attracted to small calves.*

*Ely has a great deal of growing, developing and learning to do before he becomes a large bull in his prime, but in the meantime a romp in the swamp is very satisfying.*

Opposite: *A bull crosses one of Amboseli's flooded pans at dawn. When a bull is actively seeking females he spends a considerable amount of time travelling in and outside the Park in his search.*

## April and May

The rains continued with renewed vigour in April and May, the months of heaviest rainfall, and it became difficult to get around in Amboseli. The old lake basin is the lowest point around and parts of its surface are very hard, and therefore rainwater has a tendency to just sit on the surface. At times it almost appeared to be reverting to a lake. Nevertheless, Norah and Soila braved the flooded roads and muddy terrain to keep us posted.

Typically of the homebody EBs, they did not venture far during the height of the rains, nor did they join the big aggregations very often. Ely was very active, playing vigorously and exploring away from Echo. Ely's main allomother was still Enid who was rarely more than a metre or so away from him.

Towards the end of April I went down to Amboseli to carry out routine administrative tasks and decided to visit the EBs. On 28 April, when Ely was exactly two months old, I drove out into the sodden park between the pools of standing water. I toured the EBs' usual haunts near the Serena plain and Ol Tukai Orok. By good luck I found them on the edge of the woodlands, just as they were entering an area that had turned into a marsh.

I parked next to the edge of the water and began to do a census of the family. As I was ticking off the members, an extraordinary thing happened: Echo turned at right angles to the direction she was moving in and walked straight over to the Land Rover. She stopped so close to my driver's door that I could have reached out and touched her, and stood quietly looking in at me. I talked softly to her because the elephants are familiar with our voices and become more relaxed when they know the people in a vehicle. When I had arrived she and a few others had started secreting from their temporal glands and by the time she reached the car the sides of her face were streaming with tear-like liquid. This behaviour is a sign of social excitement used, for example, during greetings. I could only suppose that our presence nearly every day for two and a half months had made us almost as much a part of her daily routine as she had become of ours. She didn't vocalise or signal in any other way, simply seeming curious and 'friendly'. She then moved to the other side of the car and stood looking in the passenger window.

Ely had gone off with Enid and Elspeth when Echo came over. While all the elephants had put on weight, Ely had grown tremendously in the one month. I watched him as he pushed and shoved Elspeth, trying to initiate a game. Then, several minutes after Echo had turned and moved on in her original direction, Ely suddenly spotted the Land Rover. As soon as he saw it, he left his companions and came straight over. He was a little more cautious than he had been a month ago, reaching his trunk out towards the vehicle from a metre or so away. A few moments later he got up his nerve, came closer and lightly touched the door with the tip of his trunk. When he grew bored and wandered off, I was surprised to see him plucking up blades of grass here and there, and chewing on them. Most calves do not even try to start feeding on vegetation until they are between three and four months old.

This encounter made me look forward even more to the dry season when Martyn and I would once again become a part of the rhythm of the EBs' lives.

# THE DRY SEASON

## *June to early November 1990*

### *The Early Dry Season: June to late September*

By June the rains had ended, but Amboseli was still green, and the vegetation continued to grow, fed on the moisture remaining in the soils. It was the beginning of the cool months in East Africa; in July and August the days are overcast and temperatures rarely reach 80°F (27°C) in the daytime and frequently drop below 50°F (10°C) at night. June is less predictable; some days are hot and sunny, while others are cold and gloomy. The elephants too are unpredictable, not having settled down into their dry season routine.

Martyn and I arrived back in Amboseli late in the afternoon of 12 June to be greeted with the news that there was a dead elephant in an area called Njiri. The next morning we drove there with Norah and Soila, and dozens of vultures led us straight to the body. It was the carcass of an adult male who had been dead for a few days. The once magnificent animal was reduced to rotting flesh and exposed bones and smelled exceedingly unpleasant. The park's rangers had already removed his tusks, which turned out to weigh 13 kilograms (29 pounds) each, indicating that he had been a fairly large bull. I shooed away the vultures

*Elephants prefer fresh grass, but in the dry season after the grass has been eaten down they turn to other vegetation. Echo is feeding on a large palm frond while Ely investigates what his mother is doing.*

On the days that the EBs stayed out towards the mountain, Martyn and I took the opportunity to focus on the lives of the males, particularly their sexual cycle of musth and retirement. Bulls begin coming into musth when they are in their late twenties, but they do not have regular cycles until they are nearing 40. The sexual cycle is a yearly one, at least in Amboseli. Generally the large males over 40 spend three to four months in musth and then eight or nine months of the year in retirement leading a very peaceful, somewhat solitary life.

My colleague Joyce Poole studied the sexual activity cycle of males and found that, when they are not in musth, Amboseli males retire to bull areas, of which there are three. Two of the areas, one to the west and one to the south-east, are on the periphery and outside the park, and are not often used by the females and calves, or only at night. The bulls living in the third area in the centre of the park, tend to feed in the very deep swamps which the family groups do not use. Thus, when a bull is not in musth, he remains more or less segregated from the cows and calves.

In my more frivolous moments I think of the bull areas as all-male clubs. The males in retirement hang out with a few buddies or move about on their own, feeding a lot, and getting plenty of rest so that they build up fat reserves for the three or four busy months of musth ahead. I can sometimes almost picture them sitting around in leather armchairs reading *Wall Street Journals*.

When a bull comes into musth he makes a strikingly different impression. Musth is similar to rutting behaviour in deer, in that males exhibit physiological changes, become aggressive and pursue females. However, in most deer, the does are only receptive for a

*The magnificent M22, who is around 50 years old and the third largest bull in the population, stretches for a palm frond way out of reach of even the biggest females.*

certain period of the year and all the stags in a region come into rut together at this breeding season. The stags, with their newly grown horns, posture and roar, fight other males, and try to herd and mate with females, all in a matter of weeks. Elephant females tend to come into oestrus during and after the rainy seasons, but the breeding period covers at least eight months, and females can be receptive in any month of the year. Therefore, the bulls' cycles are not synchronised and, at any point in the year, there will be some bulls in musth.

There are 177 adult, independent males in the Amboseli population. Of these, 26 are over 35 years old and are the prime breeding males. At the pinnacle of this group are five huge males: M13 (Iain), M126 (Bad Bull), M22 (Dionysus), M45 (Patrick) and M7 (Masaku). Their musth periods are spaced out from each other so that they are rarely in competition, which helps prevent dangerous conflicts. Bulls in musth have been known to kill an opponent.

The second largest bull in the population, M126, was in musth when the EBs were going off to the mountain. Unfortunately, we could not risk trying to film this male. He was given the name Bad Bull because he is extremely aggressive and feared by all the elephant researchers. He will go as far as 200 metres (650 feet) out of his way to threaten and charge us. We always carry out essential observations of him from a place with a clear escape route and otherwise give him a wide berth.

Just as all the researchers have favourite family groups, we also have favourite bulls. At the top of the list is the third largest male in the population, the magnificent-looking M22. He is about 50 years old, and probably weighs 5–6 tonnes and stands about 3.4 metres (11 feet) at the shoulder. His tusks are very wide at the base and sweep out and down then up again. His popularity stems both from his stateliness and the fact that he is amazingly tolerant when he is in musth. Far from terrorising us, he does not even acknowledge our presence. The only accommodation he makes is to walk around our vehicle rather than through it, displaying even less interest in us than in a bush which at least provides something to eat.

M 22's musth period covers January to early April, which is a very good slot because numerous females come into oestrus during the months following the short rainy season. Earlier in the year Martyn and I had admired M 22's adeptness at finding females at the crucial point in their oestrous cycle when they were most likely to be ovulating. He moved very busily back and forth across the park, guarding and mating with a female in Kitirua in the west on one day, and then appearing beside a different oestrous female in Olodo Are in the east on the next day. It was an impressive display of tracking skill and timing which, I estimated, earned him at least a dozen calves.

Now in his retirement phase, M 22 was living in the bull area in the centre of the park, which meant that we saw him frequently. He wandered about with a slow, purposeful stride, feeding on palms or acacia trees. Being so tall, he was able to reach succulent bits, such as dates and pods, which the cows and calves could not get. In addition, his strength allowed him to pull branches off the large trees. He could strip the bark off even the smallest of them in a feat of coordination that was a pleasure to watch. He would chisel up a piece of thin bark with his tusks. Then, holding one end of the branch with his foot and grabbing the loose bark with the 'fingers' of his trunk tip, he would pull the bark off in one long piece, place it in his mouth and eat it. Sometimes he went off to Enkongo Narok swamp near the swimming pool and disappeared into the dense papyrus in water over 2.5 metres (8 feet) deep. Occasionally he was joined by younger bulls who appeared to be warily attracted to the very large males. If a family group was around, he might feed near it but would not show any interest in the females.

In early July, our days with the males ended. The EBs started coming into the park

Overleaf: *The large AA family, another favourite of the research team, crosses the pan in a long column on their way to Enkongo Narok swamp. In their daily routine the elephants come into the swamps in the morning and move out into the surrounding bushland in the evenings.*

every day again, and doing things other than sleeping. Even more fortuitous, they were spending all their daytime hours in the area of the Ol Tukai Orok woodlands in and around my camp. There were four or five families in the population that were very habituated to the tents and people in the camp, and would come up to the periphery to feed on the grasses and palms. Two of these families, the TAs led by their matriarch Tuskless, and the EBs, would come right in and feed around the tents and shower, even venturing among the laundry hanging from the lines behind the kitchen. Their fearlessness allowed them to get the last of the good grasses, without having to compete for it with the rest of the population.

Having the elephants right in camp meant that we could observe them from a different perspective from the one we had in the Land Rover. One of the first things I noted was that Ella's breasts had shrivelled to one-quarter of their size when she was lactating. Her daughter Emma, now three years and five months old, did not appear to be attempting to suckle any longer. Therefore, Ella's next calf, due in about six months' time, would not have to compete for its mother's milk.

We were particularly delighted to have excellent views of little Ely. He was four months old, and growing and developing very fast. In late April, when I had first seen him feeding, he could pluck up one or two blades and put them in his mouth but was not feeding on vegetation seriously. On 9 July, when the family was next to my tent, I saw Ely making much more determined efforts to obtain grass, chew it and swallow it. He managed fairly well, although his trunk did not have quite the strength or coordination needed for many of the clumps. As I watched, he twirled his trunk around and around a bunch of grass, got a good grip and then pulled. The grass broke off but fell to the ground and he had to scoop it together with his trunk. He then brought it to his mouth grasped in the 'fingers' on the end of his trunk. The next clump he tackled was bigger and tougher, and would not give. He wrapped his trunk around it tighter and pulled again and again without success. Finally, he 'cheated' and simply knelt down and bit the grass with his teeth.

On this day only 13 of the 15 EBs were present. The missing pair, Eric and Emo, had been sighted by Norah and Soila with Tuskless and the TAs on one day and with the AA family on another. These adventurous young males were exploring new terrain and testing out their social status. While Emo had been coming and going ever since his mother had died, it was the first time we had recorded Eric leaving the family.

A few days later, Martyn and I reluctantly left Amboseli for another couple of months, he to return to the UK and I to go to Nairobi. Again, Norah and Soila kept us in touch with the EBs as well as monitoring the whole population. From them we learned something of Eric and Emo's movements.

On 14 July they saw Ella and her two younger calves with Eric and Emo, but separated from Echo and the others. On 23 July, Ella was reunited with Echo, and Eric and Emo were absent. There were two more sightings of the EBs at the end of July, five during August and one in September. Eric was present every time and Emo on all but two. Emo was spending over 50 per cent of his time with the EBs, indicating that he was not yet ready for independence. Despite his somewhat insecure position as a pubescent male without a mother, he still appeared to need Echo's leadership and the companionship of his relatives.

## *The Late Dry Season: late September to early November*

I returned to Amboseli on my own on 29 September and found a dry and desiccated park. There had been no rain for three months and the famous, powdery alkaline dust of Amboseli had settled over the vegetation bordering the roads, giving everything a dull, dry appearance. The air was hazy with the dust and Kilimanjaro appeared through it as a faint blue-grey outline far in the distance. By midday dozens of dust devils were swirling around the plains. The grass was reduced to a stubble out on the plains and was well cropped down at the edges of the swamps. The grazing animals were concentrated around the park's two major swamps, Longinye and Enkongo Narok, and around the smaller waterholes in Kitirua and Ol Tukai Orok, including the ones near my camp. Wildebeests,

zebras and elephants came into the camp, some feeding boldly on the grass right under the thatched roofs. Two male zebras seemed particularly at home when I arrived. One was an old stallion who had presumably given up the struggle to keep a harem of mares and the other was a young male with a strange spotted pattern who was probably not ready to try to secure females yet. They walked confidently on the paths between the tents, barely getting out of our way when we passed them. The 20 or more wildebeests that entered the camp each day were more nervous. Every time one of us appeared out of a tent, they panicked and went stampeding off, only to return a few minutes later. Tuskless and the TAs arrived nearly every day at noon and rested under

Left and below:
*At the height of the dry season there is little left to eat except for the vegetation growing in the swamps. The elephants wade right in up to their ears and feed in the swamps for hours; however, some take time out for recreation.*

the tree in the centre of the camp. As long as we did not move fast they paid no attention to the resident humans but they did take notice of strangers. Other elephants fed on the palms and around the small swamps at the periphery of the camp.

In the open glade just to the south a variety of species converged to drink and feed, including warthogs, bushbucks, buffaloes, giraffes, impalas, a rhino or two and our resident pair of lions. At night we could hear the lions roaring, plus the sounds of hippos, baboons, leopards, hyenas and jackals. With so many animals in and around it, the camp resembled a barnyard. Our once-green lawn was dug up and covered in dung, which I was sure would be beneficial in the long run but did not look very attractive.

Having concentrated on the EBs for most of the year, I felt out of touch with the rest of the elephants in the population. Therefore I decided to spend my time until Martyn arrived carrying out censuses on as many families as possible and taking photographs to update the recognition file. On the morning of 30 September, I was setting out to start on these tasks in the east when, right at the entrance to the camp, I came across 12 of the 15 EBs. The three missing members were Ewan, Emo and Eric. The rest of the family were feeding on the huge fronds of the *Phoenix reclinata* palms. These plants never looked very appetising but clearly had some nutritional content. After about 15 minutes, Ewan arrived from a small swamp to the west. When I left them, there was still no sign of Eric and Emo, but they could have been hidden behind the palms.

Over the next week, I had an enjoyable time reacquainting myself with the rest of the elephants. Then Martyn arrived in Amboseli on 15 October and, after a day of preparations, we set out to find the EBs on the 17th. Of course, when we wanted them, they were not at the entrance waiting for us. We searched from 6:30 till 12:30 and started again at 16:30. About half an hour later, we finally spotted the long graceful curves of Echo's tusks emerging from a giant palm at the southern edge of the Ol Tukai Orok woodlands. Soon we recognised Ella with her head stuck deep in another palm, and Erin and Eudora feeding on grass farther back. A closer survey revealed that all the EBs were present except for Emo. As we watched, the family came out of the woodland and started across the open pan. A little later two young males emerged from the palms and these turned out to be Emo and his friend Eugene from the EAs. They crossed on a parallel path, not exactly with the family but not truly on their own either.

That night there was lightning towards the mountain and a smell of rain in the air, and the following morning we woke to see a light coating of snow on Kilimanjaro. It was a lovely and welcome sight, bringing hope of a good wet season. Generally in Amboseli, the short rains do not come until November, but sometimes they start as early as mid-October. The earlier the rains come the better they usually are.

For the next few days, the EBs and the other families that shared their clan area followed a typical late dry season routine, spending the major part of their day feeding in and around the swamps. The EBs usually arrived at the swamp edge or their favourite patches of *consimilis* grass by dawn and did not leave for their night feeding and sleeping area outside the park until after sunset.

By this time of year, food normally became scarce and the elephants showed signs of a poor diet. However, the ones we encountered looked fine. The adults were beginning to look a little bony around the shoulders and pelvis, but they were not unduly thin. Many of the calves, especially the ones that were still suckling, continued to be butterballs, with a quilted pattern produced by fat puffing out the skin between the wrinkles. There was very little play among the calves, though, and all the elephants were moving slowly, presumably to conserve energy.

When the EBs went deep into the Enkongo Narok swamp we could not follow them, but when they went into Ol Tukai Orok we were able to stay with them for most of the day. The 21 October was one of the days that Echo led her family into the woodlands. They slowly moved through the trees, feeding as they went, and arrived at a small pond. All the elephants drank, including Ely whose drinking skills were most impressive. Now nearly eight months old, he was able to suck the water up with his trunk, carry it to his mouth, lift his head and pour the water into his mouth, hardly spilling a drop. While the others went off to feed on the surrounding palms, Ely stayed at the water's edge continuing

*Elspeth, Ely and Ella's calf, Esau, drinking with various degrees of proficiency: Elspeth at two and a half only loses a few drops, Ely at 15 months dribbles a respectable few drops, and Esau at five months spills more than he swallows.*

to drink. Eventually he appeared to get bored and started splashing the surface with his trunk and spilling water that he had sucked up.

In the meantime, Echo had managed to dig out a heart of palm with her tusks, which is a difficult task, and one she seems to specialise in. She was standing by herself, obviously relishing her feast, when M22 started to walk through the glade. He literally did a doubletake when he smelled Echo's palm heart. He stopped short, made a right-angled turn and headed straight for her. M22 is nearly a metre taller at the shoulder than Echo and probably weighs about twice as much and I assumed that if he wanted her palm heart, he would get it. I underestimated Echo. When she saw that M22 was coming, she picked up the heart and ran off with it. Ely saw his mother hurry away and, quickly trying to join her, ran directly into M22's path, which sent him into even more of a panic. A brief moment of chaos ensued, with elephants going in all directions. The end result was that M22 gave up his pursuit and ambled off in a dignified manner.

Apart from such competition over food, there is usually little interaction or interesting behaviour to observe among elephants in the late dry season. Families tend to move on their own and may even split into subgroups. There are rarely any females in oestrus, only one or two males are in musth and there are usually no births between late August and late December. Thus it came as a great surprise to witness, on the following afternoon, an event that revealed new insights into the nature of elephants. We had spent the morning of 22 October with the EBs, and at 16:30 we set out to join them again by a route that took us out on the plain to the east of our camp. There we saw a small group of four elephants, which was strange because they would normally be in the swamps or woodland at that time. Although they were half a kilometre away, I could tell from their postures that they were disturbed – their heads were held high and their ears were raised and tense. As I watched, three of the elephants moved off to the east towards Longinye swamp leaving the largest animal behind. I drove along the road towards them and saw that the large animal was the 'right one-tusked' female, Grace of the GBs. The three individuals that had walked off were her calves: Gwen (11 years), Gail (eight years) and Garissa (three years and eight months). Next to Grace was a small pale object. I was just focusing on it with my binoculars when Grace bent down and, with her tusk hooked under it and her trunk holding it from above, lifted it in the air and carried it towards the other elephants. Then I saw that it was a tiny calf. Grace moved rapidly about 20 metres (65 feet) with her head held high and her tusk stuck straight out, until the calf slipped out of her grasp and dropped more than 1.5 metres (5 feet) through the air, landing hard on the ground. The others must have heard something because they all turned round and came running back to Grace, and milled about with much rumbling and earflapping.

I spoke to a driver who said that the elephants had been there since morning when Grace had apparently given birth. The calf had been out in the hot sun all day, as well as falling at least once from a considerable height. I thought it must be dead, and left the road to drive over and check. The elephants were somewhat alarmed and defensive on our arrival, but soon ignored us. About a minute after we got there, we realised with a sickening feeling that the calf was still alive. Grace's oldest daughter, Gwen, tried to lift it and the calf, a female, twitched and let out a weak groan. The scene brought back disturbing memories of Ely's first day, but this time there could not possibly be a happy ending.

The calf lying on the ground looked about half the size of a normal newborn. I doubted whether the pitiful little creature had ever stood and suckled. It was a strange greyish-pink colour rather than the healthy dark grey of a new calf, and was bleeding slightly from the eyes, mouth and genitals. From its size and colouring, I concluded that it was born prematurely. I later looked up the oestrus records and, although that sighting was not conclusive, it suggested that Grace had been in oestrus in May 1989 and was due to have a calf in March 1991. Therefore this calf was probably about four months premature.

Grace and her older calves were all extremely distraught. They frequently rumbled contact calls and one or two of them would set off towards Longinye only to turn round and come back after going 10 or 20 metres (33–65 feet). I marvelled at the bonds between mother and calf, and between the older calves and their mother. The other members of

*Grace carries her premature and dying calf towards the seclusion of the woodlands. In the end she carried it over half a kilometre and hid it deep in a clump of palms.*

the GB family were probably within vocal distance, and food and water were nearby, but the juveniles remained, thirsty and hungry, on the open plain. Those bonds must be very beneficial to have evolved to that extent.

A pair of jackals was circling at a distance of about 50 metres (160 feet). The older elephants kept raising their heads and taking threatening steps towards them. Gwen tried several more times to lift the calf by gently nudging it with her foot and wrapping her trunk around it. As soon as it made a sound, Grace pushed Gwen aside and bent down to it herself. Three times over the next hour she lifted it on to her tusk and carried it until it dropped to the ground with a horrible thud. Each time she headed towards the woodlands of Ol Tukai Orok near my camp. Although I had read reports of females staying with their dead babies and carrying them, I think in this case, Grace was stimulated to carry the calf and not leave it because it was alive and every once in a while moved or gave a weak cry. As we were leaving them, well after sunset, Grace picked up the calf again and managed to carry it another 30 metres (100 feet).

The next morning we went out before dawn to find that Grace and her calves were no longer on the plain. We searched around the area and spotted Gwen and Gail at the edge of the palm thickets of Ol Tukai Orok. When we had driven over to them, we could make out Grace and her three-year-old, Garissa, inside the palms. By further manoeuvring the car, we could just see the tiny calf on the ground beside them. Grace had carried the calf over 500 metres (1600 feet) to the seclusion and cool of the thick palms. It was an amazing feat of dexterity and determination.

We thought that the calf was dead, but could not see well enough to be sure. In the course of the morning, there were frequent rumbling calls. Grace barely moved from the calf, only going out of the palms briefly three times. She was followed each time by Garissa, who had been trying to suckle the previous day and had been refused. On this day, Grace allowed her to drink. At noon Grace disappeared and we took the opportunity to go up to an opening in the palms and look in. The calf was lying on its brisket, no longer breathing. The ground around it was very dug up indicating there had been a great deal of disturbance in the area. Fifteen minutes later Grace and the others came back, having been to the swamp to drink. They took up their vigil once more and stayed near the dead calf for the rest of the day.

We spent the following day with the EBs, but checked on Grace when we went in and out of the camp. On the second occasion she was away from the calf and we could see that it was partially eaten. It was probably the jackals that had got to it. Lions or hyenas would have finished the carcass unless interrupted by Grace. On 25 October, three days after the birth, Grace was still in the area. She was no longer standing over the calf, but was going back to it from time to time.

We sighted the GBs on 27 October and 2 November, both times without Grace and her calves. It was not until 7 November that I recorded the whole family together again. Thus Grace had spent at least three days guarding her dead calf and had been separated from her family for two weeks. I wondered how much of that time they were in vocal communication with each other. We know that many of the rumbles that the elephants make are of very low frequency, too low for human hearing. These infrasonic calls carry great distances, possibly as far as 10 kilometres (6 miles). It could be that Grace was in fairly regular contact with the rest of her family. Indeed, while Grace was with the dead calf we heard elephant calls from her direction. We can recognise and describe many of the sounds that elephants make, but we do not yet know what messages they are conveying. I could only wonder whether Grace relayed any of the stress and disturbance she was undergoing.

Towards the end of October, rain clouds had started building up every afternoon, marching in from the east. On the 30th and 31st there was rain all around the Amboseli basin, on the slopes of the mountain and on the higher ridges to the east, but none fell in the park. Then on the afternoon of 7 November we had a brief storm of tremendous wind accompanied by only a little rain. Still, with only 300 millimetres (12 inches) of rain falling on average during the year, every drop counts. We woke on 8 November to a fresh clear day with everything looking sparkling and bright, having been washed clean by the rain. It was a day that we had set aside for paperwork and we forced ourselves to stay in the camp. Had we not done so, we might have missed a second fascinating yet sad event.

Kadzo, the Ph.D. student, had left camp early and returned around 11:30 to report a sick elephant among the AAs, a big family with 22 members. She had first noticed the young female at about 9:00, when the AAs were on the northern edge of Ol Tukai Orok. Astrid, the 11-year-old daughter of Alison, was kneeling down, urinating a lot, and appeared to have a very bad stomachache. Kadzo went off to do her work and came back to the family around 11:00. By then they had moved across the pan to the edge of Enkongo Narok swamp, leaving Astrid far behind. Her mother, Alison, kept going back to her, apparently urging her to come along.

From what Kadzo told us, I thought that Astrid might have an intestinal blockage or some other digestive disorder. However, similar behaviour I had seen once before prompted me to go to my tent and get out the records of oestrus and mating. I discovered that Astrid had been seen in oestrus on 16 December 1988, just over 22 months before when she was one month short of 10 years old. Although this would be young to start breeding, it was possible that Astrid was about to give birth.

Martyn and I leapt into the Land Rover and headed for the swamp. There we found most of the AAs feeding in the swamp and on the shore. The 28-year-old adult female Alison and her two-year-old male calf were standing next to Astrid who was lying down in the mud and water. I had known Alison since she was 10 years old and watched her grow up to have calves of her own. Astrid was her second-born and her first to survive to maturity. For the next hour, Astrid stayed there, occasionally raising her head or standing up and lying down again. From the little we could see, she might have been in labour or she might have been ill. Then at 13:50, Astrid came out of the swamp. Her vulva was hanging down, covered in mud, and a small lump protruded below her tail. That clinched it: she was in labour.

This was only the third birth that had been witnessed in the history of the project, and I watched Astrid's behaviour very carefully. After coming out of the swamp, she moved to a clump of *Salvadora persica* bushes and beat them with her tusks. She was

*In the early morning light, the elephants create an aura of mystery and timelessness as they feed amongst the classic umbrella trees of the savannah.*

holding her tail off to one side and urinating frequently, appearing agitated. Then she knelt down on her hind legs, straining several times. A few minutes later, she moved north with her mother about 30 metres (100 feet), picking leaves from bushes and eating a bit. Soon she started ripping apart a bush again, and I wondered whether this might be a reaction to the pain. At 14:09, Astrid lay down, but Alison rushed over to her rumbling and she got back up again. After another few minutes she was straining again, nearly kneeling.

Over the next couple of hours, she repeated these activities in varying order many times. Alison stayed close by but stopped encouraging her to stand after a while. Both elephants rumbled at each other and may have also been in vocal contact with the rest of the family, who had moved away, still feeding. By 16:40 the bulge below Astrid's tail seemed more pronounced and slightly lower, but otherwise there was little change.

The following extract from the detailed notes I took covers the next half hour.

**16:44** Kneels down in squatting position again, really straining now.

**16:45** Still in squatting position, holding quite still. For a first time mother she does not seem as agitated as I would have expected.

**16:46** Down on all four legs like a dog. Then rolls over partially on her side. Amelia [another adult female from the AAs] and three calves approach from the south. Exchange of rumbles between Amelia and Alison.

**16:50** Astrid stands up. Tail high up in the air. More rumbles from Amelia. Think the foetus is quite far down, part of it at least half way. Alison comes over to Astrid, reaches trunk towards her. Alison's calf arrives as well.

**17:05** She's been squatting quite a lot. Several long squats. There is now a bit of blood coming from the vagina and we can see the full length of the foetus in the birth canal.

**17:06** Squatting again. Her anus is pushed way out and the birth canal is tremendously distended. Other elephants from the family approaching. Alison staying close to her.

**17:09** She's kneeling down again on her back legs, straining. Part of it is still high up. The mass of the foetus still seems to be up below the anus.

**17:11** She just squatted again and I thought I saw the foetus slip down quite fast.

**17:12** Back up, no longer squatting. Main bulge still up by her tail.

**17:13** Squatting again down on her right rear knee. Alison staying close by.

**17:15** Stands up. There's very little blood, just a few drops. She's kicking backwards. Her whole backend is protruding out about a foot.

**17:22** Calf born.

The actual birth happened very quickly. At first, Astrid was partially obscured by a bush, and we could just see one hind foot and then another sticking out of her vulva. By good fortune, she then came out into the open and stood next to where we were parked. She gave one last push and the foetus was propelled forward with great force. It shot forwards, hind end first, and landed on its back. While its hindquarters up to the middle of its body were bare, the head and shoulders were covered in the foetal sac. Attached to the sac around its forehead was the placenta. The umbilical cord was wrapped around its chest. In the only other birth I had seen before, the calf struggled from the moment it was born. This calf lay still.

It was a large male calf with dark healthy looking skin. As soon as it dropped, Astrid backed over it and moved away with her trunk and ears out, looking very alarmed. Her mother, Alison, immediately came over to inspect the calf. She reached her trunk out and shook her head with a loud slap of her ears against her neck – a typical gesture of elephant 'disapproval'. She moved closer and gently nudged the calf with her foot and tried to lift it. The calf continued to lie still and we realised then that it was dead.

Virtually all elephant births at Amboseli take place at night and I suspected that Astrid had started in labour the night before or as long as 24 hours before. Perhaps it was a long labour because it was a breech birth or because the calf was large and Astrid was relatively young. Whatever the reason, I thought the calf had died as a result of the long labour, probably smothered by the umbilical cord around its chest.

While her mother tried to lift the calf, Astrid stood about 12 metres (40 feet) away, looking dazed. About eight minutes after the birth, she went back over to the calf, smelled

*Eleven-year-old Astrid of the AA family finally reaches the last stage of her long labour as the calf's feet begin to emerge.*

it and rumbled. In the meantime, Alison moved off in a purposeful manner heading north. Over the next 15 minutes two more females from the AA family arrived and smelled the calf. They seemed to know right away that it was dead, becoming quiet and hesitant in the way that elephants do when they come upon elephant bones or carcasses. Then the adult female Audrey arrived with her own calf, which was no bigger than the dead calf. She greeted Astrid by reaching her trunk towards her mouth, and smelled the calf. Afterwards she turned her back on it and very gently reached backwards and touched it with one hind foot, a gesture I have seen made to other dead elephants before. Audrey turned back round to face the calf and, bending down, ripped open the foetal sac with one

*The calf shoots forward, hind feet first and lands on its back with the fetal sac and placenta covering its head.*

of her tusks. Usually a calf kicks in the sac and females will help the mother remove the membrane. This time there was no movement and Audrey gave up after one tear.

Astrid was standing quietly nearby, sometimes picking up sticks and throwing them in a form of displacement activity. Then she came closer to the dead calf but still appeared to be frightened of it. At 17:55 a second wave of animals from the large AA family began to arrive. Astrid became more alert and, after being greeted by her relatives, started secreting from her temporal glands. I found it interesting that the secretions flowed in such social situations and not, for example, in the stress of labour.

By 18:00 Astrid seemed less exhausted and more disturbed. She stood right next to

# DROUGHT

## *November 1990 to March 1991*

### *November and December*

During the remainder of November and most of December I was in Nairobi and relied on Kadzo, Norah and Soila for news of Amboseli. More rain came in November and the park turned green, but early in December the rains ended. On adding up the figures I found that the total rainfall for the short rainy season was a disappointing 66.2 millimetres (2.6 inches). In good years as much as 200 millimetres (7.8 inches) of rain fell in Amboseli during October, November and December. In some years, such as 1990, the 'between the rains' months of January and February received extra rain, and I hoped this would happen in 1991.

On 17 December, Norah came across the EBs while carrying out censuses of the family groups and bulls. All the members were present, apart from Emo. They were in Olodo Are, probably having moved out of their dry season home range in response to the rainfall. A few minutes after sighting them, she realised that there was a tiny calf with Ella. On closer inspection she saw that it was a male calf and estimated that he was about

*Amboseli is famous for its fine alkaline dust which becomes a familiar feature during the dry season and an all-pervasive presence during a drought.*

five days old. Although he had been born a few weeks earlier than we had expected, he did not look particularly small. He was not as big as Ely had been at birth, but this was probably just as well. Ella's calf looked normal, active, and healthy.

I went to Amboseli with several friends for Christmas, and was pleased to see that the grass had grown up in the camp and all looked well. During my short stay I tried twice to find the EBs but had no luck. Norah reported that there were few elephants in the park, and those that were tended to gather in large groups in Olodo Are. She had last seen Echo and her family on 21 December in Longinye among a group of 55 elephants.

## *January to March*

Martyn arrived in Kenya on 8 January and we returned to Amboseli on the 11th. As at the beginning of 1990, the sky was a clear blue and Kilimanjaro seemed closer and more magnificent with no clouds to shroud it. January is my favourite month in Amboseli. The park is green, the elephants tend to gather in large herds, there is usually a lot of oestrous behaviour and musth activity, and baby elephants almost appear to be dropping out of the sky. The only nagging worry I had this year was that the clear skies held little promise of the much-needed extra rain.

On the following day we toured Echo's favourite haunts and, as usual, could not find her. Each time we returned after being away, it seemed to take us a couple of days to get back in touch with her routine. It was not until the next evening that we located her and her family just emerging from the Ol Tukai Orok woodlands. Everyone except Emo was there and they all looked well, including Ella's new calf whom I named Esau.

Over the next few days we saw the EBs regularly, and Emo was absent every time. He seemed to have made a definite break. His move towards independence was confirmed on 18 January when the EBs were feeding just at the edge of the camp. Echo and the family had been in the area since early in the morning. At midday, Emo arrived with another family, the CBs. I thought he would go over and join his family, and I wondered how they would react to him. However, he did not even approach them. He left the CBs and wandered off to the south on his own, never having been closer than 100 metres (330 feet) to his family. He looked too small at 10 years old to be on his own and I was concerned about whether he would make it through the vulnerable teenage years. I would probably only have intermittent sightings of him as he grew and matured through his teens and 20s, until eventually he settled into a bull area and became a large breeding male with a regular routine.

A week later, on 25 January, we had an encounter that gave me some insights into the lives of medium-sized independent males. That evening we were driving back to camp when we saw two bulls out on the open pan to the east of Ol Tukai Orok. I do not know the bulls nearly as well as the females, partly because I see them less regularly. Also, the males grow and change more rapidly than the females, and their ears seem to get more tears and holes in the course of time. I usually have to refer to the photographs on file in order to identify a bull. I did not immediately recognise either of these bulls, but something familiar about one of them made me stop the Land Rover.

They were both handsome, leggy bulls in their mid-twenties. By this age, the males are 30 centimetres or so (about a foot) taller than the biggest adult females, and their tusks are already thicker and heavier than those of any female. Despite his size and much thicker tusks, one of the bulls looked remarkably like Emo. I checked the file and confirmed that he was Little Male, Emo's older brother, who had left the family in 1983. I had not seen him, or at least had not been aware of seeing him, since 1989. I found it interesting that the sibling resemblance was so striking. It was also noteworthy that his companion was Ezra, who had left his natal family, the EAs, around the same time as Little Male. These two males had frequently been together when they were still in their families and were continuing to associate several years after independence. The records showed that they were not together consistently but that there was a tendency for them to be in the same bull group. Possibly males form stronger bonds than I had thought.

By Little Male and Ezra's age, bulls are just beginning to try to compete for females.

They are what is known as 'sneaky copulators'. In their mid-twenties, males are not big enough or strong enough to fight outright for oestrous females, and thus they have to adopt other strategies to secure matings. One technique is to find an oestrous female and mate with her before the big males find her. Another is to hang around when she is being guarded by a large musth male in the hope that he will be distracted by, for example, a potentially dangerous rival. While the big male is busy chasing off another big male, the sneaky copulators rush in and attempt to mate with the female.

We were keeping an eye on the older males too during this season because we wanted to film a male in musth. We came across two musth bulls in January, M10 and M132 (Chris). However, our first choice for the role was the striking and highly tolerant M22. In 1990 we had admired his skill in tracking down oestrous females during his musth period and spent an enjoyable few days with him in June during his retirement phase. This year we wanted to follow his musth activities in more detail. We were reasonably hopeful because M22 had a fairly predictable sexual cycle. We had musth records for him going back to 1977, and these showed that he had been in musth from January until March or April for the past 13 years.

This January we found him still in his bull area which, conveniently, was the Ol Tukai Orok woodland and Enkongo Narok swamp, the same general range that the EBs used. He showed none of the obvious characteristics associated with musth. He was usually on his own or in the vicinity of other bulls or family groups, and did not appear to be interested in females. On looking carefully at him I thought he seemed thinner than bulls

*The Amboseli elephants share their range and their resources with a host of other grazing species including zebras and wildebeests. During hard times there is serious competition for the remaining vegetation.*

*Emma with her new brother, Esau. Enid had monopolised Ely, rarely letting anyone else look after him, but when Esau was born Emma finally had 'her own' calf to take care of.*
Opposite: *At dawn, a large bull is already up and trying to find the tastiest morsels.*

*The young female Ute is tested by Sleepy, one of Amboseli's biggest males and here in full musth. He clearly finds her of considerable interest as he assesses the hormones in her urine with a special gland in his mouth.*

*Another musth male, Thor, mates with Penelope, the matriarch of the PA family; her family rushes over to participate in the mating pandemonium.*

but I thought he would probably do so again. We waited for several hours until, at 13:25, Odette initiated the mating sequence herself. She moved off looking back over her shoulder in the classic oestrous walk. All the other bulls had started to converge on her before Patrick woke up and realised what was happening. He quickly set off after her, simultaneously releasing his penis from the sheath. Since Odette seemed to know just what she was doing, he did not have to chase her very far. When he caught up, he laid his trunk along her back and she stopped walking. Then, with his chin on her backside, he levered himself up on his hind legs and rested his front feet just behind her shoulders. His 1.2 metre (4 foot) long penis, with muscles allowing directional control, had curved into an S-shape. He hooked the tip of the penis into her vagina and with a thrust upwards his long organ was deep inside her. She cooperated by standing still and there was no apparent movement during the 45 seconds until he dismounted. Then the real excitement started. Odette lifted her head, opened her mouth and started making very deep, pulsating, rumbling calls. At the same time most of her family arrived, screaming, trumpeting, rumbling, roaring and bellowing in a display called 'the mating pandemonium'. Her family reached their trunks towards her mouth, her vulva and the fluids on the ground, while Odette turned and touched Patrick's penis three times with her trunk.

Odette's post-copulatory rumbles and the mating pandemonium of her family could be heard over a wide area. Joyce and I have speculated that these calls broadcast the news that there is a female in oestrus to draw in more males and increase the chances that the biggest, most dominant male around will find and mate with her. While females of other species generally advertise their availability, it is unusual for whole families to participate in the mate-attracting effort as they appear to do in elephant society. Odette was already with one of the 'best' bulls in the population and thus she and her family had been fairly successful. There was a possibility, though, that their calls might attract an even 'better' bull in musth at that time, such as M13. However, by the following day Odette was out of oestrus, and we could expect a new calf in the OAs about 656 days later, sometime in April 1993.

Having successfully filmed oestrous and mating behaviour our goal was once again to find the EBs each day and spend time with the family. The EBs cooperated by being easy to find, but we often had difficulty getting to them. In contrast with our experiences during the months of drought, Martyn and I were being continually diverted by exciting elephant behaviour everywhere we went. There seemed to be females in oestrus around every corner and almost each day brought a new bull into musth. We found newborn calves in many of the groups we encountered and the families were gathering in spectacular aggregations. Fortunately, the EBs were joining aggregations and we could often both be with them and have the chance of seeing other elephants' behaviour as well.

It was a week after Odette's mating that we were seriously distracted from the EBs once again. We had made our usual start at sunrise and at 6:40, we found a large, loose herd of cows, calves and bulls coming down through the *Acacia tortilis* strip and out on to the grassland. There were about 200 animals in the aggregation including, on the far side, the EBs. We took a while to get over to them because I carried out censuses of the other families on the way. When we arrived at 7:10, we saw that they were near the EAs. Enid was separated from the rest of the EBs, looking somewhat agitated, and after a few moments I realised why. Evangeline of the EAs was in oestrus, probably the early stages, since she was oestrous-walking away from several young males who were interested in her. At nine years old, Enid was young to start sexual cycling but could come into oestrus. In any event, she was following Evangeline around, fascinated by the activity.

A bull in musth was close to, but not guarding, Evangeline. This bull, estimated to be 40 years old, was named Beach Ball because he was particularly round in appearance. We had been with the family for less than five minutes when a second male in musth arrived. This was Lexi, the one-tusked bull who had so ignominiously retreated from Patrick. Lexi was about two years younger than Beach Ball but was similar to him in size. This time Lexi did not seem to be intimidated. At 7:15 I was writing some notes when Enid suddenly started screaming. I looked up and saw that she was in between Lexi and Beach Ball who were both standing tall with their ears spread and folded, threatening each other. Lexi

lunged towards Beach Ball and Enid screamed again. Other animals arrived as a result of the first scream, including Emo and Eric who stood submissively with their heads very low, watching the two musth bulls. Enid managed to extricate herself and moved off to a safe distance.

It is not unusual to see males of all ages sparring. They usually reach trunks towards each other, place them in each other's mouths, feel around each other's heads and tusks, and then gently start to push on one another. The movements in sparring are generally slow and languid, although they can escalate into more aggressive twisting and shoving. A true fight between bulls is a much rarer and very different affair involving far less physical contact and much more manoeuvring.

Beach Ball and Lexi were obviously having a serious fight despite the fact that they were not yet touching. Instead, they were manoeuvring continuously to keep facing each other at all times. If one bull turned sideways, the other could tusk him in a vulnerable area or knock him down and possibly kill him. Therefore they kept 15–20 metres (50–65 feet) apart, constantly turning and adjusting their positions with their hind legs. When they moved farther apart one or both would bash a bush or lift a large log and toss it around. Sometimes one would kneel and dig his tusks into the ground in a display that seemed to demonstrate what he would like to do to his opponent.

It was not until nearly an hour after Enid's scream that the bulls had their first clash. They came together with a tremendous thud and clank of ivory, and great clouds of dust rose from the impact. Each attempted to twist the other off his feet, but they were evenly matched and quickly backed off, resuming their lethal dance. At 8:40 they clashed again

*When two musth males of similar age and size meet they may have a serious fight during which one could be badly injured or even killed. These fights are frightening to behold and much different in character from the almost languid sparring matches.*

Above and right:
*Over the 18 months the rhythm of our days was determined by the EBs as we followed them from sunrise to sunset. We had become a part of Echo's world and sometimes were privileged to feel that she and her family accepted and even welcomed our company; she taught us much about elephants, about leadship, about maternal care, survival and about some of the concepts that are not supposed to be applied to animals: patience, loyalty, love and joy.*

the fighting bulls the day before. I was doing a census of the EBs when the EA family passed close by. Emerald's '89 female calf broke off from the group to join the EB calves and Ely went enthusiastically out of the family circle to meet her. After a brief exchange of trunks to each other's mouths, he started butting her with his head, and she turned and moved off. Ely put his head on her back and tried to mount, but Emerald's calf was a year older than Ely and just too tall for him. Undeterred, he reared up on his hind legs and had nearly got his feet on her back when she moved, leaving him suspended in mid-air. He took several steps forward on his back legs, looking totally ridiculous.

It was particularly interesting to watch Emerald's calf and Ely after all the adult interactions we had seen over the last two weeks. In his play, Ely had acted like a typical male calf. From very early on, male calves are more likely to leave their mothers to play and their behaviour during play is noticeably different from that of the female calves. They do more head-to-head sparring and engage in more rough and tumble play. If one calf mounts another, it will almost invariably be a male calf who does the mounting. Females tend to play running and chasing games, and those involving attacks on imaginary enemies. Both are practising skills they will need as adults: for the males, fighting and mating techniques; and for the females, strategies for protecting their calves and their families.

Ely went chasing after Emerald's calf and, even though he was now 15 months old, Enid went after him. She literally herded him back to Echo, pushing him with her trunk and tusks. He was soon off again, this time to join Ella's calf, Esau, and once again Enid followed him. She was a tireless allomother, and I felt sure she would be a good mother when she had her first calf, which could be in two or three years' time.

The elephants were soon all around my tent, ignoring me as I sat in my chair under the thatched roof. On one side, Echo, Eliot, Erin, Edgar and Eudora continued to rest under the tree. Erin was due to have a calf in a few weeks' time, and was slow and heavy. She had nearly weaned Edgar who was not at all pleased. He was only two years and eight months old, which was exceptionally young to have to go without milk. He stuck close to his mother, trying to suckle as soon as she went to sleep or got distracted, but she was on the alert and quickly stopped him. Eudora stood right next to Echo, completely integrated in the family despite her mother Emily's death. Far from becoming peripheral as I had feared, she seemed to have developed very strong bonds with Echo. I suspected that she would come into oestrous soon since she had shown some early signs of it in late May. If she did conceive in the next couple of months, she would give birth to a new calf when Elspeth was four and a half years old – much better family planning than Erin.

On the other side of my tent, Ella was feeding while six-month-old Esau played with Ely and Elspeth under a palm. Elspeth was lying down, and Ely and Esau were climbing on her and falling off. The other 'girls', Edwina, Eleanor, Emma and Enid, were standing nearby, keeping an eye on the younger calves. Eric and Ewan had joined Ebenezer and Ethan of the EAs, and they were all chasing each other through the palms.

Soon, however, most activity stopped and the members of the EBs slowly gravitated to Echo. They moved to the shade of the tree and gathered around her. The bigger animals lowered their heads, draped their trunks over their tusks, and slowly flapped their ears. The little calves flopped down and were quickly sound asleep. Even a few of the bigger calves lay down, turning into great grey boulders in the grass. Echo stood in the middle surrounded by her close relatives, each bonded to her in a different way, all dependent on her knowledge and wisdom, which had brought them through the good times and the bad.

There would be more tragedies and joys for the EBs, but for today all was peaceful, all was well.

# INDEX

*Page references in italics refer to illustrations*